The Inward Pilgrimage

SPIRITUAL CLASSICS
FROM
AUGUSTINE
TO
BONHOEFFER

Bernhard Christensen

AUGSBURG PUBLISHING HOUSE
Minneapolis, Minnesota

To Gracia
and to Nadia, Marya, Marina, and Sonya
and in memory of Naomi

THE INWARD PILGRIMAGE

Copyright © 1976 Augsburg Publishing House

Library of Congress Catalog Card No. 75-22725

International Standard Book No. 0-8066-1510-9

Scripture quotations unless otherwise noted are from the Revised Standard Version of the Bible, copyright 1946, 1952, and 1971 by the Division of Christian Education of the National Council of Churches.

MANUFACTURED IN THE UNITED STATES OF AMERICA

Contents

Prolog

"There is a river whose streams make glad the city of God." This beautiful metaphor from Psalm 46 suggests the place of the spiritual classics in the life of the Christian church. Arising in many ages and many lands, these writings nourish the life of the Christian as a clear-flowing stream nourishes the trees along its banks. Offering life-giving spiritual food, they truly "make glad" the hearts of those who dwell in the city of God.

But what *is* a spiritual classic—or, to use a more familiar term, a devotional classic? How do a few books, from among the thousands of religious books written, come to have this singular distinction? All spiritual classics seem to have at least five essential characteristics in common:

1. First of all, they are not concerned basically with doctrine or ethics, but with *the soul's life with God*. Their aim is not chiefly to instruct the mind, but to lift the heart toward the Eternal.

2. They have stood the test of time, having long been read and loved without losing their appeal.

3. They are ecumenical in outlook, appealing to Christians of many times and many denominations. Each book reflects its own age and circumstances of writing, yet to a remarkable degree "speaks to the condition" of Christians everywhere.

4. They deal especially with the great theme of prayer, so central to all religious experience. As Douglas Steere, well-known author of books on the inner life, has said:

> Nearly all these great books relate themselves to prayer. They lead up to prayer, they make prayer necessary, they almost force us into prayer. . . . [They] touch upon the areas of life that prayer deals with.[1]

5. Finally, they are books not to be read once and laid aside, but to be often reread and meditated upon. They are not passing acquaintances, but abiding companions on the way of life.

Every age of the church has produced examples of these treasures of spirituality. With the passage of time, however, and with the rise of divisions within the church, even some of the finest of the classics have come to be neglected. A major purpose of this book is to introduce to today's reader a number of the greatest classics portraying the soul's "inward pilgrimage." The ones here presented are but a few, yet a chosen few, with representation from each of the three epochs of the church's history: ancient, medieval, and modern. Since it is the author's hope that the reading of this volume will often be a stepping-stone to reading the classics themselves, I have chosen books which are readily available—in most instances in paperback editions. Judged by the five criteria listed above, these sixteen books are all worthy of being known by Christians of all denominations.

What greater reading privilege could there be, aside from reading the Scriptures themselves, than to share in the companionship of those through whom we have been given so rich a spiritual endowment? If it is a good thing to cultivate the fellowship of contemporary spiritual Christians, it is an equal enrichment, by means of the printed page, to "walk through the centuries" in the company of good friends of God.

Such a walk leads inevitably to a vision of the manifold variety of spiritual experience. As the colors of one spectrum of light can blend into numberless patterns of beauty, so the one light of faith reveals itself in a multitude of varying life-patterns, all beautiful The gifts and graces of the Spirit have come to expression in widely different forms in different ages of the church, but an essential unity pervades them all. The piety of an English Baptist differs from that of a Scandinavian Lutheran; an American Quaker's prayer life will not be the same as that of a Spanish Catholic. Yet the widely divergent patterns of faith all reflect the one life in Christ. And learning to know the spiritual life as it has been lived among men and women of other cultures and other churches can add immeasurably to our own inner pilgrimage.

Furthermore, these books have a vital contribution to make to our practical life day by day. Dorothy Ranaghan, writing in *As the Spirit Leads Us,* describes the aim of Christian spirituality as "a plan, a means, an attempt to find a way of living every day in a growing union with God."[2] The spiritual classics, while building upon the enduring realities of the Christian faith, will give such guidance. Though some have been written in a time different from our own, they still speak to our modern need.

Yet these classics do not foster a spiritual individualism. While they do not all stress with equal emphasis our participation in the life and activities of the church, the type of devotional life recommended is nearly always church-centered. The "life together," portrayed by Dietrich Bonhoeffer, is clearly rooted in the Word and the sacraments. St. Francis seeks the approbation of his bishop. The Russian Pilgrim attends the public liturgy at every possible opportunity. The spiritual classics, rightly read, will lead us closer to the heart of the church, to its worship and sacraments, to its fellowship and world-wide mission.

Finally, to read the spiritual classics is to explore the "mansions within," so well described by St. Teresa of Avila in her

Interior Castle. Her "mansions" are arranged in a definite order of spiritual progression, but the spirituality unveiled in the classics depicts the soul's life at many levels, often with no attempt at structural portrayal. From its own unique approach, each book reflects and illumines the inward pilgrimage and urges the reader to "enter into himself" in quest of a fuller life with God.

Each chapter in this book seeks to characterize the spiritual setting out of which a particular classic originated, to give at least a vignette of the author's life, and then to summarize the main teachings of the book, including representative quotations. *The Inward Pilgrimage* aims primarily to be a helpful introduction to the reading of the masterpieces themselves. At the same time, it is the author's hope that the reading of these chapters will in itself be a meaningful devotional experience, and that it may lead to the further step of sharing the reading and discussion of the classics with others—seekers, friends, and kindred spirits. For spiritual truth is most fully possessed only when it is passed on.

THE SETTING:	4th-century North Africa and Italy
THE BOOK:	A renowned Church Father reflects on the transforming grace of God and man's unending quest for truth

The Confessions
St. Augustine

I wandered upon the broad way of the world, but you did not forsake me.

The Confessions of St. Augustine, one of the greatest autobiographies, is also one of the most widely known and loved of all Christian books. Written about a dozen years after its author's conversion to the Christian faith, it tells the story of his childhood and youth, his early departure into a life of gross sin, his years of philosophical searching, and his gradual return to God and to inner peace. In form the book is one continuous heart-searching prayer, as the author bares his soul to God and to his readers. He quotes the Scriptures constantly, but also draws upon the wisdom of secular literature and philosophy, in both of which fields he was well-schooled. Abounding in passages of keen intellectual analysis and profound spiritual insight, the Confessions portrays both the depths and the heights of human experience. "No writer," says John K. Ryan, "ever went deeper into his own character and deeds, passed keener judgments upon himself, or revealed himself more fully and more humbly to others." [1]

At the same time the *Confessions* is a continuous hymn of praise to the glory of the Creator and Redeemer of mankind. Its eloquent presentation of Christian truth and of the soul's longing for God has been likened to great organ music; and like great music the book can be heard, or read, again and again, ever opening up new vistas of beauty and meaning.

Aurelius Augustinus was born in Tagaste in North Africa in 354 A.D. His mother, Monica, was a Christian, but his father was not. Augustine was not baptized as a child, but his mother's prayers surrounded him from his birth. Nevertheless, his years of childhood and youth were unhappy. Looking back upon them, he recalls the unreasonableness and cruelty of his teachers, his utter distaste for some of the subjects he was forced to study, his yielding to temptations such as stealing—just "for the fun of it" or from fear of his companions' ridicule. His parents seemed more concerned for the development of his brilliant mind than for the formation of his character. Lacking any inward stability and surrounded by temptations, Augustine rapidly degenerated. The violent spectacles of the amphitheatre enthralled and debased his mind. During his student days in Carthage he began to wallow in the filth of careless youthful lust.

The *Confessions* shows, however, that even during these bitter and sin-soiled years, there were glimpses of light, upward urgings, deep dissatisfactions. His reading of the *Hortensius* by Cicero awakened a thirst for true wisdom, which never left him. Despite his moral aberrations he early became a successful teacher of rhetoric. But his soul was not at peace. For years he went from one philosophy to another. Manichaeism, a dualistic religion that exalted both good and evil, held him captive for years, but lost its hold upon him when one of its leading teachers proved to be outwardly attractive but inwardly shallow. For a time he was allured by astrology, but the counsel of a good physician friend liberated him from that snare. The teachings of the Platonists were helpful, but not enough to give him the peace which he desired.

Gradually his mind and heart were drawn back toward Christianity. When he began to study the Christian doctrines in earnest, he found himself at first both attracted and repelled. On the one hand, he felt that the simplicity of the Scriptures could not compare with the nobility of Cicero's style and thought. And yet, he writes, he saw

> something within them that was neither revealed to
> the proud nor made plain to children, that was lowly
> on one's entrance but lofty on further advance, and
> that was veiled over in mysteries.[2]

The Scriptures seemed to call for a childlike spirit, whereas he as yet disdained to be a little child. And always his sins of the flesh held him fast. He had lived with a concubine for years, and he could not bear the thought of giving her up. Sometimes he prayed, "Make me pure—but not yet!"

Little by little the vanity and emptiness of the world's wisdom became clear to him.

> What did it profit me that I, who was then a most
> wicked servant of base lusts, should read and under-
> stand all the books of the liberal arts? . . . I found
> joy in these books, but I did not know the source of
> whatever was good and certain within them. I had my
> back to the light.[3]

When he was about 30 years old, Augustine, weary of the disreputable conduct of his students in Carthage, went to Rome. But teaching there presented other irritating problems, so after a short time he accepted a position in Milan. His mother and some of his friends accompanied him.

In Milan he came under the influence of the great Bishop Ambrose, whose example and preaching came to be of critical importance in Augustine's life. He was challenged by the Bishop's noble life, and by his continence. The sermons of Ambrose were of particular help in clearing away many false interpretations of Scripture. "The letter kills, but the spirit gives life," he would constantly emphasize, as he showed that a great deal of the Bible was to be understood *spiritually* and not literally.

As Augustine listened, his mind was convinced. But as we read of his conversion experience in the *Confessions,* we see that his heart ultimately found rest not through human philosophy or learning, not even through the arguments of persuasive preaching, but through personal contacts with a group of men with a living faith in Christ. But first both his mind and heart had to be convinced of the central message of the gospel:

> I sought for a way of gaining strength sufficient for me to have joy in you, but I did not find it until I embraced the mediator between God and man, the man Christ Jesus, who is over all things, God blessed forever.[4]

Acceptance of the Incarnation became the key to the door of faith into which he was soon to be ushered by the voice of a little child.

Some months after coming to Milan, Augustine, deeply aware of his need of spiritual counsel, sought out Simplicianus, an older Christian who was also a friend of Bishop Ambrose. From Simplicianus he learned the story of Victorinus, a great pagan teacher who in his old age became a Christian and made public confession of his faith. As Augustine listened to this story about Victorinus, he says, "I was on fire to imitate him." But he did not yet make the crucial decision. He was still, as he says, "in both camps," likening himself to a man beginning to be aroused from sleep, who still says drowsily, "Let me be for a little while longer."

Then one day a visitor, a fellow-African named Ponticianus, came to the home of Augustine and his friend Alypius. Ponticianus was a Christian, and when he noticed a volume of the Epistles of St. Paul lying there, he was led to tell how two friends of his had been converted through reading the life of St. Anthony the hermit. As Augustine heard how Anthony had forsaken all to live a life of utter devotion to God in the desert, he was deeply moved. When Ponticianus left, his heart was in a torment of indecision, torn between the call of the flesh and the call of God. Leaving Alypius, he went out into the garden adjoining the house, and wept bitterly.

Suddenly, in a moment of silence, he heard the voice of a child in an adjacent yard repeating the words: "Take up and read; take up and read." It seemed to him that God was speaking directly to him. Here are Augustine's words describing what followed:

> I hurried back to the spot where Alypius was sitting, for I had put there the volume of the apostle when I got up and left him. I snatched it up, opened it, and read in silence the chapter on which my eye first fell: "Not in rioting and drunkenness, not in chambering and impurities, not in strife and envying; but put you on the Lord Jesus Christ, and make no provision for the flesh, in its concupiscence." No further wished I to read, nor was there need to do so. Instantly, in truth, at the end of this sentence, as if before a peaceful light streaming into my heart, all the dark shadows of doubt fled away.[5]

This story of Augustine's conversion is recorded in Book 8 of the Confessions. For him it marked the great transition from death to life. Now a new life opened. Book 9 tells how he resigned his professorship, how with a group of friends he spent some months in retirement and study, how at Easter in 387 A.D. he was baptized by Bishop Ambrose together with his son Adeodatus and with Alypius, and how together with his mother and his brother he journeyed to Rome enroute to his home in Africa. Monica's prayers for her son had been more than answered. Now she was ready to bid farewell to this earth. "What am I doing here any longer?" she asked.

Before telling of his mother's death, Augustine pays beautiful tribute to her as both a faithful wife and a devoted mother. He speaks to God about her, calling her "that handmaiden of yours who brought me to birth, both in her flesh so that I was born into this temporal light, and in her heart, that I might be born into eternal light." [6] He tells of her great patience in the hardships and wrongs she suffered at the hands of her husband, whom she at last won to Christ; and of her consecrated life as the "servant of the servants of God." Gratefully he points to the secret of her noble life: "She had you," he says to God, "as her inward teacher in the school of the heart." [7]

One of the most beautiful passages in the *Confessions,* and indeed in all religious literature, is Augustine's account of his conversation with his mother shortly before her death, as they stood by a window looking out over a garden in Ostia. They speak of the meaning of "eternal life," the life set free from all the burdens and shadows of time. As they converse, they rise ever higher in thought and spirit, until, as it were, they are in the very presence of the Eternal. It is not strange that Monica was ready to bid earth farewell. Earlier she had wanted to be buried by her husband in Africa, but now she simply said, "Nothing is far from God." [8]

Books 8 and 9, where Augustine tells so personally and in detail of the central crisis of his life, are no doubt the most fascinating part of the *Confessions,* but the entire work is a rich mine of spiritual truth and insight. The whole story of Augustine's long pilgrimage from sin and doubt to purity and faith and newness of life is filled with example and precept for every Christian. The last part of the *Confessions* (Books 10 to 13), dealing chiefly with intricate philosophical and theological problems, is perhaps less helpful to most readers. And the record of the last half of Augustine's long life until his death in 430 A.D.—as Bishop of Hippo, as scholar and writer, as fearless controversialist and gentle pastor of his people—all of this lies beyond the scope of the *Confessions.* But the book still remains the best introduction to the greatest of the Western Church Fathers and among all his writings the most direct source of spiritual help for the lay reader.

Almost every page of the *Confessions* abounds in words of wisdom which have been the inspiration of Christians ever since they were first written. Many passages deserve not only to be meditated upon, but to be made a permanent treasure of our hearts. Who among all earth's writers can speak as eloquently and profoundly as St. Augustine on the greatest themes—God and man, life and death, sin and grace, time and eternity? Once read and pondered, passages like the following can scarcely ever be forgotten:

> You have made us for yourself, O Lord, and our heart is restless until it rests in you.[9]

> Give what you command, and command what you will.[10]

> Too narrow is the house of my soul for you to enter into it: let it be enlarged by you. It lies in ruins; build it up again.[11]

> Too late have I loved you, O Beauty so ancient and so new, too late have I loved you! Behold, you were within me while I was outside: it was there that I sought you, and rushed headlong upon these things of beauty which you have made. You were with me, but I was not with you. They kept me far from you, those fair things which, if they were not in you, would not exist at all. You have called to me and have cried out, and have shattered my deafness. You have blazed forth with light, . . . and have put my blindness to flight. . . . I have tasted you and I hunger and thirst after you. You have touched me, and I have burned for your peace.[12]

> Wheresoever I found truth, there I found my God, truth itself.[13]

The *Confessions,* which begins by praising God for his greatness and his gifts, closes with a sublime prayer for the greatest gift of all: that the peace of God, "the peace without an evening," may be ours forever:

> O Lord God, give us peace, for you have given all things to us, the peace of rest, the peace of the sabbath, the peace without an evening. This entire

most beautiful order of things that are very good . . .
is to pass away. For truly in them a morning has been
made and an evening also. But the seventh day is
without an evening, because you have sanctified it to
endure to all eternity. . . . We also, after our works,
. . . may rest in you in the sabbath of eternal life.

Then also you shall rest in us, even as now you work
in us, and so will that rest of yours be in us. . . . But
you, O Lord, are ever at work and ever at rest.[14]

It is a high vision of human destiny to come to the soul of a
man—a vision of unending fellowship with the living God, he
in us and we in him; and we, in whom he has worked here in
our earth years, now become also the place of his eternal rest.
The storms of sin and the tempests of time are past. The Lord
God Omnipotent—the Lord of Omnipotent Love—reigneth, for
ever and ever!

THE SETTING:	4th- and 5th-century Egypt and the Near East
THE BOOK:	The life and wisdom of the hermits of the desert

The Desert Fathers
Helen Waddell

Their denial of the life of earth has been the incalculable enriching of it.

One of the strangest movements in the entire history of Christendom was the flight, during the fourth and fifth centuries, of tens of thousands of Christians into the hermit life of the deserts of Egypt and the Near East. There they lived in solitude or in small groups, raising or receiving only the barest necessities of life, and spending their time chiefly in prayer and in an earnest quest for a deeper life with God. When we read of them, we may at first be tempted to turn away in utter unbelief, even in disgust, thinking that the whole movement was mere fanaticism—as it has, indeed, often been derided by the world. But if we pause to become better acquainted with these desert-dwellers, their ways and their wisdom, their defeats and their victories, we find that they have something of unique and enduring worth to say to us.

Such a closer acquaintance has now been made possible through the publication of *The Desert Fathers,* by Helen Waddell, an English classical and medieval scholar. By careful editing of selected passages chosen from the masses of material which have been preserved, and by the addition of helpful notes, the author opens the door for today's readers to enter into a "fellowship of solitude" with these men and women of the desert of long ago. In addition to these solitaries of the wilderness, Miss Waddell introduces a number of other striking figures, not strictly hermits but exhibiting a similar spirit of discipline and great gentleness. Included too are the strange stories of a number of women redeemed from sin through the witness of the saintly hermits. The desert scene was stern and unrelenting, but in its midst blossomed memorable flowers of grace and virtue.

St. Anthony of Egypt, though not the first hermit, set the pattern and drew multitudes of other men and women to the desert. The historian Gibbon called Anthony's life and influence a vast tragedy—but there are values that historians can overlook.

Anthony was born in Coma in upper Egypt, about the year 251. His parents were wealthy, earnest Coptic Christians, and the boy Anthony was carefully nurtured in that faith. When he was only twenty, his parents died, leaving their land and wealth to him. One day in church he heard the priest read Christ's command to the rich young ruler: "One thing thou lackest; go, sell all, and give to the poor." He felt that the word was addressed to him, and he obeyed. Leaving behind all his possessions, he began, not long after, the hermit life in desert solitude which was to continue for about eighty years, with but few interruptions. He died when more than a hundred years old. By that time thousands upon thousands had followed his example. He himself had been the counselor of bishops and emperors. His friend, the great Athanasius, wrote his biography. It was soon translated and brought to the West where, in the strange ways of divine grace, it became an important link in the conversion of St. Augustine.

From the narrative in the *Confessions* it is clear that it was Anthony's willingness to forsake everything in his quest for life with God that made such a revolutionary impact upon Augustine. And as we read about the men and women of the desert it is the same startling fact that stands out: they were convinced that *communion with God is a priceless treasure.* It was this communion, above all, that solitude gave them. Outward deprivation and discipline were but a means to that end. Life with God was the pearl of great price; to possess it they gladly sold their all.

Miss Waddell observes how difficult it is for modern man to recognize the claim of these spiritual ventures that summon all our reserves of strength and endurance in a solitary quest for the Eternal One. We readily grant, she says, that the dedicated soldier, the arctic explorer, the artist in the South Seas, the pioneer in space research, shall endure unmeasured self-denial, shall risk everything—even life itself—for his own satisfaction or for the enrichment of mankind. Only God is not deemed worthy of such sacrifice!

The dispelling of this error is the major message that sounds from the hermits of the desert. It clearly rings in the beautiful words of Paulinus of Nola, a French nobleman and ex-senator who had himself renounced worldly success to become a humble priest,

> The shows and forms of things, . . .
>   despising the loveliness
> Soliciting for ill our mortal eyes.
> The present's nothing: but eternity
> Abides for those on whom all truth, all good,
> Hath shone in one entire and perfect light.[1]

Sustained and guided by that light the men and women of the desert gladly faced the terrors both of the life and the last enemy, Death.

The writings which Miss Waddell has gathered give many pictures of the stern, rugged settings in which the monks lived out their life-long quest. A typical passage from the "Lives of the Fathers" takes us to Scete, one of the most isolated but most famed centers of monastic life:

> The place in which the Holy Macarius lived was called Scete. It is set in a vast desert, a day and a night

journey from the monasteries on Nitria, and the way
to it is to be found or shown by no track . . . but one
journeys by the signs and courses of the stars. Water
is hard to find. . . . Here therefore are men made perfect in holiness; . . . yet their chief concern is the love
which they show to one another and towards such as
by chance reach that spot.[2]

This paragraph strikes a revealing note, very important for
understanding the hermit's manner of life: the scene is desolate
and harsh, but within it the fires of fraternal love glow brightly.
Numerous references bear witness to this important fact. One
writer gives us this vignette of brotherhood in action:

They dwell dispersed throughout the desert and separate in their cells, but bound together by love. . . .
Quiet are they and gentle. . . . They have indeed a
great rivalry among them . . . it is who shall be more
merciful than his brother, kinder, humbler, more
patient.[3]

Ironically, we hear most often of the extremists among the hermits—such as Simeon Stylites spending many years atop his pillar.
But these were the rare exceptions. Most of the desert-dwellers
were earnest men of God, even though their concept of following Christ lacked a vision of the world-affirming and world-serv-
ing qualities proclaimed in the New Testament. They saw only
"in a mirror dimly" the meaning of freedom in Christ, but their
passionate purpose to follow the will of God cannot be ques-
tioned. Says Abbot Abraham:

We are not ignorant that in our land there are fair
and secret places where there be fruit trees in plenty
. . . and the richness of the land would give us our
daily bread with very little bodily toil. . . . But we
have despised all these and with them all the luxurious pleasure of the world: we have joy in this desolation, and to all delight do we prefer the dread
vastness of this solitude.[4]

For thousands this stern choice became the gateway to a life of prayer and utter self-giving love to both God and man. John Cassian, one of the notable fifth-century writers, who had spent some years among the hermits in Egypt, and to whom we are indebted for so much of our knowledge of the desert Fathers, gives us this picture of the "reward unspeakable" that came to some of those who braved the path of desolation in quest of the greatest riches of all—the moment of mystic vision when

> beyond sound of voice or movement of the tongue or any uttered word, when the mind is narrowed by no human speech, but . . . all its senses gathered in one round, leaps like a fountain toward God, discovering in one brief particle of time such things as cannot easily be spoken, . . . when all love, all longing, all desire, all seeking, all thoughts of ours, all that we see, all that we say, all that we hope, shall be God.[5]

It is to this strange world, where physical desolation and aloneness become the setting for a life of ardent prayer and unceasing love and service that *The Desert Fathers* introduces us. The whole book is a series of kaleidoscopic pictures of human life reduced to utterest simplicity as far as "daily bread" is concerned, but ever richly provided with the bread of the soul. Perhaps few of us will read the entire book, and so succeed in envisioning all the changing scenes. But even gleaning in scattered portions will yield a rich harvest also for the contemporary Christian.

Among the treasures brought to us in these writings are the tales, many very strange and some no doubt apocryphal, of moving spiritual experience: of Paul the First Hermit, deep in the desert, saintly and humble, visited by St. Anthony as he neared death in his 113th year, buried with the assistance of friendly lions; of the holy Paphnutius, who by his humility and his keen understanding of souls was able to lead men of many different callings to God; of Abbot Abraham who donned other garments and went without fear into the bedroom of a brothel to win his niece back to Christ; of the blessed Pambo who "made so light of silver and gold that verily he seemed to have fulfilled the Lord's commandment"; and of Lady Melania whom Pambo taught that generosity is truest when concealed. The presence and work of the Holy Spirit stand clearly revealed in stories such as these, and many others similar to them.

The "Sayings of the Fathers" make up a major part of Miss Waddell's book. Here the wisdom of the monks is distilled in brief paragraphs, or even single sentences, revealing a great depth of spiritual understanding, and frequently, too, a profound psychological insight into the motives, the moral struggles, and the sins of men. For monks remain men. Statements like these are as valid in the twentieth century as in the fifth:

> The Abbot Anthony said, "Who sits in solitude and is quiet hath escaped from three wars: hearing, speaking, seeing; yet against one thing shall he continually battle: that is, his own heart." [6]

> The abbess Matrona said, . . . "It is better to have many about thee, and to live the solitary life in thy will, than to be alone and the desire of thy mind be with the crowd." [7]

> The Abbot Macarius said, "If in desiring to rebuke any one thou art thyself moved to anger, thou dost satisfy thine own passion; in saving another, lose not thyself." [8]

> The holy Syncletica said, "A treasure that is known is quickly spent: and even so any virtue that is commented on and made a public show of is destroyed. Even as wax is melted before the face of fire, so is the soul enfeebled by praise, and loses the toughness of its virtues." [9]

> A certain brother had sinned, and the priest commanded him to go out from the church. But Bessarion rose up and went out with him, saying, "I, too, am a sinful man." [10]

An old man said, "See that thou despise not the brother that stands by thee: for thou knowest not whether the spirit of God be in thee or in him." [11]

As he lay dying, Paphnutius said, "No one in this world ought to be despised, let him be a thief, or an actor on the stage, or one that tilled the ground . . . for in every condition of human life there are souls that please God and have their hidden deeds wherein he takes delight." [12]

The abbot Mathois said, "The nearer a man approaches to God, the greater sinner he sees himself to be." [13]

In addition to the moving tales and the capsulized wisdom, a third important element in these writings is the many memorable characters to which they introduce us. We can mention only a few.

There is Macarius the Good. One of the incidents told about him is that he came to his hut one day to find someone thieving there. Macarius stood by like an obliging stranger, and then helped the intruder load his animal, and finally led him out, making no noise. "But Macarius," the brethren said, "was like God, who shields the world and bears its sin." [14]

There is Bishop Nonnus of Edessa, attending a bishops' meeting in Antioch. During their gathering Pelagia the courtesan rode by, dressed in jewels and splendor. While the other bishops turned their eyes away, Nonnus freely continued to look at Pelagia, both because he admired her beauty and because her care for her outward appearance put to shame his comparative negligence in caring for his soul. And not many days later, we are told, the bishop's preaching won Pelagia's heart for Christ.

There is Benus, of whom the brethren declared "that never had an oath or lie come from his mouth, nor had any of mankind ever seen him angry, or saying an unnecessary or idle word, but that his life went by in a great silence, . . . and in all things he lived as an angel might: moreover he was of vast humility . . . and did reckon himself of no account." [15]

Beneath the stories, the words, and the lives of the desert Fathers lay the deeper reality which they ever saw and sought to communicate: the *eternal setting* which is the true environment of the human soul. It is this setting—the soul alone before its Maker and Judge—that it is so hard for contemporary man, living in a world of technology and science, to discern and experience. The desert ideal, "to be alone with the Alone," eludes us. Man becomes great, and God small. Not so for the Desert Fathers. Says Miss Waddell:

> They thought to devaluate time by setting it over against eternity, and instead they have given it an unplumbed depth. . . . The sense of infinity is now in our blood.[16]

> Their every action shows a standard of values that turns the world upside-down. It was their humility, their gentleness, their heart-breaking courtesy that was the seal of their sanctity, . . . far beyond abstinence or miracle or sign.[17]

From other writers we may learn and be gripped by other values—the joys of social fellowship, appreciation of the beauty of nature, the blessings of the Christian family, the meaning of human history, the intricate wonders of the created world. From the Desert Fathers we learn, as from scarcely any other spiritual ancestors, the riches of being alone with God.

THE SETTING: 13th-century Italy

THE BOOK: Stories and legends of "the Little Poor Man of Assisi" and his friends

The Little Flowers of St. Francis

Anonymous

Wherefore he chose to live rather for all men than for his single self, inspired by the example of Him Who brooked to die, One Man for all.

More than seven hundred years intervened between the death of St. Augustine and the birth of Francis of Assisi, whose life enkindled the most far-flung spiritual awakening that came to Christendom in the Middle Ages. Francis has often been called the greatest follower of Christ after Saint Paul. Whether so or not, it is certain that the life and spirit of "the Little Poor Man of Assisi" have had a universality of appeal and influence difficult to exaggerate. The story of how the voice of God came to him, summoning him to his life work, is told in simple words in the *Life* by St. Bonaventura:

On a certain day, when he had gone forth to meditate in the fields, he was walking nigh the church of St. Damian, . . . and, at the prompting of the Spirit, went within to pray. . . . As with eyes full of tears he gazed upon the Lord's cross, he heard with his bodily ears a voice proceeding from that cross, saying thrice, "Fran-

25

cis, go and repair My House, which, as thou seest, is falling utterly into ruin." Francis trembled. . . . When at last he came unto himself again, he prepared to obey.[1]

The whole church, through all subsequent centuries, was to feel the effects of his obedience.

Francis was born in 1182, the son of a wealthy cloth merchant, Pietro di Bernadone. As a youth he was gentle, but full of energy, zestful, and fun-loving. Among his comrades, he quickly won friends, both by his attractive personality and by his spendthrift generosity. Though never involved in the coarser vices, he became known throughout the city as a leader of youth in revelry and folly. When he was about twenty years old, Assisi went to war with a neighboring city. Francis was captured in battle and spent a frustrating year in prison. This experience, and a long period of illness which followed, led to his awakening to more serious thoughts about life and its meaning. Restless and dissatisfied, he began to search for God.

The events connected with his conversion, culminating in his hearing the voice of Christ in St. Damian's calling him to service, came when he was about 25 years old. Taking this call seriously—and literally—he sold all his possessions and gave the money to help repair the little church. But he could already see that a more far-reaching task awaited him.

As the voice of Christ had said to him, the church was falling into ruins and in deep need of renewal. The reign of Innocent III, pope at the time of Francis' conversion, is commonly called the high point of papal power. But beneath the outward splendor lay widespread corruption and utter worldliness.

Francis soon became the friend and companion of the poor and the outcast. He took a special interest in the lepers, washing their sores. One day in a dramatic gesture in the public square of Assisi, he announced that he was taking "Lady Poverty" as his bride. His father was furious when he learned that Francis had been giving away all his money, and, haling him before the bishop, threatened to deprive him of his whole inheritance. But

Francis was unmoved. He renounced his father, giving his rich clothing back to him, saying,

> Hitherto I have called thee my father on earth, but henceforth I can confidently say, "Our Father Which art in heaven" with Whom I have laid up my whole treasure.[2]

With a transfigured heart and a strange revolutionary spirit, he began challenging the ways of both the church and the world of his time, seeking to follow literally the example of Jesus in poverty, humility, and brotherly love. What he himself practiced, he began to teach to a growing circle of followers who gathered round him. His program, as he lived and taught it, is summarized in a sermon which he preached at a chapter meeting some years later. In this sermon he encouraged the friars

> to reverence and obedience to Holy Mother Church, and to sweet brotherly love, to pray for all the people of God, to have patience in the adversities of the world and temperance in prosperity, to maintain an angelic purity and chastity, to remain at peace and harmony with God and with men and with their own conscience; to humility and meekness toward all, to the contempt of the world and a love and fervent practice of holy poverty.[3]

Francis had been called to "repair the church," but he was to accomplish this not by any outward revolution, any overturning of constituted authorities, as is so clearly seen in this sermon. Rather his aim and program was to *rebuild from within*. Only then could there be a real and enduring renewal in the House of God.

Stories about St. Francis began to be written down not long after his death, and many were soon gathered into official biographies. *The Little Flowers* was written considerably later, first in a Latin text by a Brother Ugolino and then about fifty years later in Italian by a gifted but anonymous author. Though it is "the most popular of all books about St. Francis," it is not a biography nor even altogether reliable history, but rather a supplement, embellished from the loving memories of his followers, to the earlier biographies issued about one hundred and fifty years after the death of St. Francis. But so moving and convincing is the essential message and so fascinating the style of writing, that even the tales which are clearly legendary bring us vividly into the presence of the Christ-like spirit of the saint.

Early in his ministry, says a beautiful *Little Flowers* story, Francis "was placed in a great agony of doubt" as to whether he should engage in a public ministry or spend his time in a ministry devoted to prayer. Anxious to know the will of God in the matter, he did not trust just his own judgment. He sent one of his companions to ask for prayer for guidance by two of his closest spiritual friends. Both of these received from Christ the same clear answer: "He wants you to go about the world preaching, because God did not call you for yourself alone, but also for the salvation of others." [4] Francis accepted this answer with great gladness, and set forth at once with two companions, "all aflame with divine power."

In the village where he first preached, his message was so well received that all the people wanted to join the Order; but Francis told them not to decide too quickly, and in his mind he began to plan the organization of a "Third Order," to be made up of lay people who continued in their regular callings, but still followed certain religious devotions and services "for the salvation of all people everywhere."

Throughout his ministry, a strong missionary emphasis was at the heart of Francis' program; to win men to Christ was his goal and his joy. Shortly after the Order had gained approval in Rome, he himself, during one of the Crusades, set out on a mission to the Moslems. This effort did not succeed, but passing unharmed through the battle lines, Francis did have an opportunity to preach before the Sultan, the ruler of Islam, who heard his message with deep respect.

In obedience to the answer given to the intercession by his friends, Francis divided his time between the inner life of prayer and the outward life of soul-winning. Reading *The Little Flowers* one hardly knows which to admire more: the beauty of Francis' own life in Christ or the transforming influence which he had upon his followers. Of St. Francis' own Christlike qualities, one of the most outstanding was surely his humility, so well illustrated by his seeking the guidance of God through the prayers of coworkers. Many other incidents reveal the same trait. When he was asked, for example, why *he,* rather than some one else, had been selected by God to lead the movement, he answered after a moment's thought, that it was perhaps because he of all men had least to boast of in himself, and therefore God could trust him.

His humility expressed itself also in a gentle and forgiving spirit toward all men. For example, when one of the brothers, whom he appointed as guardian in his absence, drove away some robbers with angry words, Francis upon returning sent him out to find the robbers and ask their pardon. All three robbers were thus brought back to God.

This quality of gentleness was surely one secret of Francis' influence over animals, though no doubt there is much that is legendary about these strange tales. He preached to the birds, and they were quiet until he pronounced the benediction; then they flew away in good order. He took time to free some doves and make a nest for them; and while doing so won the allegiance of the young lad who had ensnared them. He calmed the fierce wolf of Gubbio, so that the people of that community no longer needed to be afraid. St. Francis was indeed an "instrument of his peace," both in the human world and beyond. Divine grace seems to have granted him "a new adjustment to the world revealed only to the singularly pure in heart."

Many *Little Flowers* tales speak with admiration of St. Francis' ability to read the hearts and understand the characters of those with whom he dealt. He knows that Brother Rufino is among the saintliest of men, "but St. Francis never said those words in the presence of Brother Rufino." [5] He reproves Brother Elias, one of the most "difficult" of his companions, for his pride.

He prophesies the suicide of Brother Giovanni (we are startled to read!). But he is gentle and kind to all, good and evil. He reads the rancorous thoughts of hatred in the mind of one who has thereby admitted a devil into the fellowship of the Portiuncula, but as soon as the sin is confessed, it is forgiven.

Such a spirit, embodying and revealing the love of Christ, could not fail to be a powerful influence on those who came into touch with him. Both his example and his words were filled with transforming power. Having enjoyed the hospitality of a nobleman and been treated with unusual courtesy, he interpreted this kindness as a signal to seek to win the man to the service of Christ. Thieves and robbers joined the Order because he dared to treat them as people. Clara Favorino, a gifted young noblewoman of Assisi, was inspired by his life-style and responded to its challenge. A little later, with his help, she founded the Second Order, for women, and thereby "cast anew a tender glory over the religious revival." Bernard, the first convert in the movement, was won through observing Francis' devoted example and prayer life. Silvester, an avaricious businessman, drawn by the wonderful generosity which both Francis and Bernard showed toward him, gave up his wealth to the Brotherhood.

And St. Francis' public ministry was as effective as his private. Here is a "typical" picture of his preaching at Bologna:

> When the entire square was filled with men and women and students, St. Francis stood up on a high place in the center and began to preach what the Holy Spirit dictated to him. And he preached such marvelous and astounding things that he seemed to be not a man but an angel. His heavenly words seemed like sharp arrows which were shot from the bow of divine wisdom and pierced the hearts of everyone so effectively that by this sermon he converted a very great multitude of men and women from a state of sin to remorse and penance.[6]

Not only Francis himself, but also the companions who gathered around him during the foundation days of the Order, made

memorable contributions to the fulfillment of the Franciscan
ideal, though the influence of Francis always was the clearly
dominant one among them all. This is strikingly portrayed in
the symbolic vision of one of the brothers, James of Massa, in
which Christ calls St. Francis and gives him "a chalice full of
the spirit of life" and says to him, "Go and visit your friars and
let them drink from this chalice." [7]

The many varieties of Christlikeness revealed in the lives of
the Little Brothers make it difficult to select any for special com-
ment. In the *Little Flowers* there seems to be a preference for
telling those whose service to the Franciscan cause was marked
by special humility and self-forgetfulness. One such was Brother
John of Penna, described as "a man of great devotion and
prayer" and "always a man with joy and peace of mind." At a
very young age, he volunteered to go on a mission to Provence,
which was then regarded as a "foreign field." When he had spent
25 faithful years there, he returned to the "home base" in Italy.
Reassigned to another field, he served there for an even longer
period, and in the same spirit. As death approached, however,
fierce temptations no doubt assailed him—as is so often the case
with God's faithful servants. But another of the inconspicuous
Franciscans, Brother Matthew, was able, by pointing to God's
great mercy in Christ, to lead Brother John out of despair into
the light of a renewed faith. Then death had no terrors for him.[8]

Concerning the saintly Brother Bernard we read that when he
was sent to Bologna by St. Francis to found a new work there,
he was insulted and ridiculed by the children in the public
square for his simple, ragged garb. When he endured this abuse
with great patience and gentleness, it so impressed a judge in
the city that he donated a house, furnished and prepared, to
the Order as a place of mission. And the judge, the *Little Flowers* says, "henceforth became a father and a special protector to
Brother Bernard and his companions." [9]

These are but a few of the holy companions to whom St. Francis gave "the chalice of the spirit of life." They typify thousands,
for the Franciscan movement grew step by step and advanced
over the whole earth. And despite the storms which have swept

over it, it still lives and serves mankind, ever challenged and inspired by the spirit of its founder.

The crowning experience of St. Francis' life was his receiving the "stigmata," the marks of the crucified Christ, in his hands and feet and side. A wealthy friend had given to the Brotherhood a lovely and rugged mountain called La Verna, as a suitable retreat for solitude and meditation. After the close of a large chapter meeting in 1224, Francis retired to this mountain, purposing to make there a long and rigorous fast. After some days, leaving behind the little group who had accompanied him, he went into complete solitude. J. O. Dobson, a Franciscan biographer, has written of that ordeal:

> It was the final contest of his faith with evil, the complete submission of his spirit to his Lord. But he knew also that ineffable joy and illumination, when it seemed that he was indeed sharing in the Eternal Life.[10]

One day, as he was praying before his little cell, there came a vision clothed in light. "The face was gracious and beautiful beyond telling, yet it was a face of suffering." [11] When the vision had passed, Francis could see that in his own body he had received the "final seal," the marks of the Crucified.

This supreme "fellowship of the cross" was the culmination of a life of hardship, affliction, anguish. Few religious leaders have had to bear more suffering than St. Francis of Assisi: suffering within, in a frail and disease-racked body; and sufferings without, in misunderstanding, rejection, and persecution. Nevertheless the dominant keynote of his whole life was joy—joy in God and in all the wonders of his creation, joy in Christ the savior and friend of sinful man. A passage in one of the Franciscan chronicles tells us that one day the saint accompanied by Brother Giles was descending the lovely wooded hillside leading down to the Marshes of Ancona. As they walked,

> Francis sang aloud in French, praising and blessing the Lord for His goodness. For they felt their hearts

overflow with fervent joy, as though they had acquired
an immense treasure.[12]

They had begun their blessed new life in extreme poverty, but
God was leading them into a part of the land where their work
would bear bounteous fruit. And so they sang.

In the lovely "Canticle of the Sun" written near the end of
his life, Francis has given the most famous expression to his joy
in God and in the creation. Among its beautiful stanzas are these:

> Be praised, my Lord, for Sister Water,
>   who is very useful and humble and chaste!
> Be praised, my Lord, for Brother Fire,
>   by whom you give us light at night,
>   and he is beautiful and merry and mighty and
>   strong.
> Be praised, my Lord, for our Sister Mother Earth,
>   who sustains and governs us,
>   and produces fruits with colorful flowers and leaves!
> Be praised, my Lord, for our Sister Bodily Death,
>   from whom no living man can escape.[13]

It is not strange that at the end, when hardship and illness had
done their work on his frail body, and one of his friends told
him that death was near, "blessed Francis was seen from these
words to derive a new joy to his mind." Calling Brother Angelo
and Brother Leo to his side, he told them to sing to him of
Sister Death. And so those two brethren sang, with many tears,
the Song of Brother Sun.

Only a few days later they carried him, at his request, down
to the Portiuncula, the first home of the Order. There they
obeyed him when he asked to be laid naked on the ground, on
the breast of Sister Mother Earth, that he might there breathe
his last breath. He died on October 4, 1226, only 44 years old—
after 20 years of earnest following in the footsteps of the Master
whom he loved. Two years later his friend and protector, Pope
Gregory IX, responded to the convictions in the hearts of tens
of thousands by enrolling his name among those "whom the

Church delights to honor," the calendar of saints. Perhaps concerning no other name on that list has there been more universal agreement throughout all Christendom, both then and now.

To read the *Little Flowers* is to be carried back across the centuries into the presence of this most unique of all the saints, and into the glad company of those whom his life had inspired and illumined. Who can lay the book down and turn away without a new-kindled desire to be a better Christian?

THE SETTING:	The Low Countries in the 15th century
THE BOOK:	Meditations and directions concerning the Christian life

The Imitation of Christ
Thomas à Kempis

All is vanity, save to love God and serve Him only.

In the fourteenth and fifteenth centuries in Western Europe, especially in the Low Countries and along the Rhine, there were strong movements which sought to promote a deeper and purer Christian life among both clergy and lay people. One of these movements, called "The Brethren of the Common Life," was centered in a famous school and community at Deventer, founded by Gerhard de Groote, a gifted educator and ardent spiritual leader. De Groote, born in Deventer in 1340, came from a wealthy family and had an excellent university education. He began what promised to be a brilliant teaching career. Then at about 35 he experienced a radical conversion, after which his manner of life was completely changed. Simplicity and devotion now became its pattern. For about three years he lived in a monastery, and then, upon the advice of the great spiritual teacher, Jan van Ruysbroek, he accepted a commission as a missionary preacher in the diocese of Utrecht. Though never ordained, he spent several years travelling, preaching against ecclesiastical abuses and calling the people to repentance, until his stern message led to his commission being withdrawn. During those years, it is said, the people of Holland were stirred toward God as they have never otherwise been. De Groote's life and preaching were, however, cut short. While bringing medical help to one suffering from the plague, he himself was stricken and soon after died, at the age of only 44. But his dedicated life had sown seeds that were to bear rich fruit in thousands of his followers.

Like their founder and leader, the Brethren of the Common Life recognized the widespread corruption prevailing in the church, and many of them boldly protested and preached against it. At Deventer and in their other communities, some of the brethren lived together in Brotherhood houses; others continued their ordinary life in the world. All of them had as their aim a higher level of spiritual life, including both a "closer walk with God" for themselves and more devoted service to their fellowmen. One of their most effective instruments for carrying out their program was the founding and conducting of Christian schools. Both in the Low Countries and in Germany, the schools of the Brethren became the most famous of their time. Albert Hyma, a distinguished historian of the movement, has given this picture of their life and activities:

> They taught and preached love, obedience, peace, and humility, fed the poor, sheltered the homeless, cured the sick, reformed monasteries, corrected abuses, and wrote books like the *Imitation*. They shared the fate of the "hidden saints," whose names seldom if ever appear in our newspapers but whose influence is often much greater than that of a heretic or a hero, or a scoundrel.[1]

The Brethren were ardent reformers but not revolutionaries. They aimed to renew the life of the church from within.

The quiet work of the Brethren of the Common Life marked, in fact, a mighty movement of the Spirit. Both through their schools and through unorganized contacts among lay groups, their influence spread from the Low Countries to Germany, Switzerland, France, and beyond. Many of the great scholars and church leaders of the time came from among their students. Among the common people their program of spiritual renewal, called the "Devotio Moderna," led multitudes into a new life of Christian love and freedom. And when, after a time, the movement lost its force and its schools one by one closed, the heart of its life—the call to penitence and faith and to a consecrated walk with God—lived on through the pages of the remarkable little book, the *Imitation of Christ.*

In the year 1392 there came as a student to Deventer a young German lad named Thomas Haemerken, later to be known as Thomas à Kempis. Seven years later Thomas entered the monastery at Zwolle, not far away, where he continued to live until his death in 1471 at the age of 91. His life as a monk might seem to us quite uneventful: studying, writing, copying manuscripts; but through it we have been given one of the most beloved and influential books ever written. In recent years, some scholars have held that Gerhard de Groote himself was the author of large portions of the *Imitation of Christ,* and that Thomas à Kempis was merely the compiler and copyist. Even if this should prove to be true, the book has still come to us through Thomas, with whose name it has been associated from the beginning. The exhortation found in the *Imitation* itself is relevant at this point: "Ask not who said this, or that, but mark what is spoken." [2]

The *Imitation* is made up of only four short "books." Three of these consist of brief meditations, prayers, and precepts concerning the Christian's life with God. The fourth is a treatise on the Sacrament of the Altar, or Holy Communion, giving pastoral guidance as to its right reception. Written originally in Latin, the book has long ago been translated into all the languages of the civilized world, appearing in an estimated total of about 6000 editions.

Yet, even so great and so beloved a book has not been without its critics. Some have said that it preaches asceticism too strongly, making it appear that Christianity consists in giving up all the joy and pleasures of life. In answer to this, it should be pointed out that it is asceticism *with a purpose* that is recommended. All life needs to be disciplined, trained. The ambitious athlete must often deny himself legitimate pleasure for a time. Christ, too, bore much of hardship and taught his followers that the way to life is narrow and often difficult. And far from presenting merely a gloomy and joyless view of life, the *Imitation* clearly points to the secret of true and abiding joy, namely, a good conscience: "If thy conscience be at peace, thou wilt never lack joy," says a key passage in Book II.[3]

Another common criticism of the *Imitation* is that its emphasis is too individualistic: we are to "work out our own salvation," but with too little concern about the social aspects of religion. These objections may have a certain validity, but no book can serve every need. The *Imitation* was not designed as a "book of common prayer," but rather as a guide for the individual pilgrim. It teaches that prayer and devotion are *good in themselves,* entirely apart from any social purpose they may serve. And its presupposition is that the individual's sincere walk with God will inevitably also nourish the roots of social good and true Christian community. It has been well pointed out that nothing in the *Imitation* would reveal the interest of the Brethren of the Common Life in education, yet their schools flourished throughout western Europe.

To offset such criticisms, we have the testimony of thousands that here is indeed a book that can minister to the needs of the human heart. Over the whole world, lay and learned, old and young, prince and prelate, have been nourished and inspired by its wisdom. Ignatius Loyola, the founder of the Jesuits, kept it always on the table in his room. Dag Hammarskjöld, Secretary General of the United Nations, made it his constant companion. Douglas Steere, one of the great spiritual teachers of today, lists the names of many who have prized the *Imitation,* and then tells how he himself, at first a reluctant reader, came to treasure its message.

The reasons for such a universal appeal are not too hard to discern when we begin to examine more closely the basic teachings of the *Imitation*. Far from being merely negative and repressive, it sets forth in chiselled perspective the great positive principles of Christian living. Its words are often deceptively simple. But they challenge the soul in its depths. In the first three books of the *Imitation* we find constant and repeated emphasis upon such central and basic "principles of Christian practice" as these:

1. *Prayer:* There is no greater good for man than prayer. It is of the very essence of the Kingdom of God. "Learn to despise all outward things, devoting thyself to spiritual things only, and thou wilt perceive the Kingdom of God come unto thee." [4] "Christ will come unto thee, and give thee His consolation, if thou prepare for Him in thy heart a worthy dwelling place." [5] This inward communion of the soul with God is the heart of the prayer-life. "The inward man He often visiteth, sweetly communing with him, and granting unto him gracious comfort, peace, and wonderful friendship." [6] The whole *Imitation* is a guide to just such a deep prayer-life. Many of its most moving passages are, in fact, prayers, in which the needs of the soul are laid open before God for his help and healing.

2. *Reading of the Scriptures:* The Bible should be read with faith and devotion. Mere argument about the Scriptures, or too much attention to "curiosity of style" can deprive us of deeper values. "If thou desire to reap benefit [by reading of the Scriptures], read with humility simplicity and faith; nor ever crave the reputation of learning." [7]

3. *Surrender of the Will to God:* God has given us our will, in order that we may yield it up to him, and thereby find true freedom. And if we ask, "How often shall I resign myself? and wherein shall I forsake myself?" the answer is uncompromising:

> Always, yea, every hour; in small things and in great.
> Thou must divest thyself of self in all things. For how
> canst thou be Mine and I thine, unless, both inwardly
> and outwardly, thou be stripped of all self-will?
> . . . Forsake thyself, resign thyself, and thou wilt enjoy
> great inward peace, Give all for all; ask for nothing;

require nothing back; abide purely and unhesitatingly in Me, and thou wilt possess Me. Then shalt thou be free in heart, and no darkness shall burden thy spirit.[8]

Chapter 37 of Book III is one of the finest statements of the Christian's secret of a happy life that has ever been written. In few places does the call of God to the soul sound more clearly, more lovingly, more compellingly.

4. *Self-Discipline:* To live the Christian life is a life-long task. We must learn to live with others, with ourselves, and with God. And this all requires discipline. We need to know ourselves, and especially our weaknesses. "We frequently do evil, and, what is worse, we excuse it. Oftentimes we are moved with passion and think it to be zeal."[9] Even our concern for others' spiritual welfare must be disciplined: "If one that hath been once or twice admonished will not yield, contend not with him, but commit all to God, that His will may be done."[10]

One of the most important forms of self-discipline is the frequent withdrawal from company in order to seek inward quiet. Most of us talk too much, and thereby "spiritual strength oozes away." "Only he that loveth seclusion may safely appear abroad without fear of hurt to his soul."[11]

5. *Humility:* Christ was meek and lowly in heart. To follow him may at times be difficult for our ego. "It is oftentimes profitable to us that other men know and reprove our faults, for thus only do we preserve our humility."[12] To hear other men praised while we ourselves are overlooked is difficult but salutary. To be opposed and misunderstood when we know we are in the right is likewise hard but healthy. The standards of humility set by the *Imitation* are high: "Think not that thou hast made any progress in the things of the spirit unless thou esteem thyself inferior to all men."[13]

6. *The Guidance of the Spirit:* For the author of the *Imitation* the possibility of clear inner direction by the Holy Spirit was very real. He says:

Moses hesitated not at all times to have recourse to the Tabernacle when beset by doubts and dangers, resorting to prayer for God's help and guidance against the iniquities of men. So oughtest thou, in like manner, to take refuge within the secret chamber of thine heart, beseeching earnestly the divine favor.[14]

Without the inward illumination of the Spirit even the sacred words of Scripture are not a sufficient guide. So he prays earnestly for "the word and light from above":

Let not Moses, nor any of the Prophets, speak to me; but do Thou speak unto me, O Lord God, Who dost inspire and enlighten all the prophets. Thou alone, without their aid, canst perfectly instruct me, . . . They speak most beautifully, but if Thou be silent, they inflame not the heart. They give the letter, but Thou only canst enlighten the understanding.[15]

7. *Love:* The greatest of Christian virtues is love. In the *Imitation* it is praised and enjoined again and again. The great "Hymn of Love" in Book III, Chapter 5, is worthy of being compared with Paul's hymn in 1 Corinthians 13, as a few excerpts will indicate:

Love is a great thing, yea, great and good beyond comprehension; love alone lighteneth every burden, and maketh the rough places smooth. For the burden it carrieth becometh like unto no burden, and everything that is bitter it maketh sweet and wholesome. . . . Nothing is sweeter than love; nothing stronger, nothing higher, nothing wider, nothing more pleasant, nothing fuller or better in Heaven or earth; for love is born of God, and can not rest save in God, above all created things. . . .

Let me sing the song of love; let me follow Thee, my Beloved, into High Heaven, and let my soul consume herself in praising Thee, rejoicing for love. Let me love Thee more than myself, and myself only for Thee.[16]

8. *Practical Judgment:* The Christian life is not an unattainable ideal. It sets high, but not impossible goals. It recognizes that our life must be lived in the midst of earth's limitations. The *Imitation* again and again points out the need for sound practical judgment in dealing with our problems. When we weary of "spiritual" activities, we are told, and lose taste for prayer and meditation, it is often a good thing to turn to bodily work for change and refreshment. Such activity, too, is the work of God. In due season the hunger for spiritual activities will return. Repeated spiritual renewal is both a possibility and a necessity all through life.

> All is not lost, although thou dost oftentimes feel thyself troubled or grievously tempted. Thou art a man, and not God; thou art flesh and not an angel. How canst thou hope to abide always in the same state of virtue, when even an angel in Heaven, and the first man in paradise, did fall? I am He that raiseth up to safety them . . . that are conscious of their own infirmity.[17]

9. *Cross-bearing:* Life for the Christian is never a path of roses; rather, it frequently involves the wearing of a crown of thorns. "Jesus now hath many lovers of His Heavenly kingdom, but few bearers of His Cross; He hath many that are desirous of consolation, but few of tribulation."[18] Christ Himself deliberately chose the way of the cross as the fundamental pattern of His life. "He that bore His own cross is gone before and showeth thee the way. He died for thee upon the Cross, that thou also shouldst bear thy cross, and, for Love of Him, be ready to die on the Cross."[19] If there had been any better way for the health of man's soul than to suffer, our Lord Jesus would have showed it by word and by example. Yet even the heaviest cross leads at last to liberation and to joy. "If thou bear the Cross willingly, it will bear thee, and lead thee to the end thou desirest."[20]

After the strenuous teachings of the first three books of the

Imitation, Book IV is a heart-searching commentary on a chief source of needed strength: the Sacrament of Holy Communion. The Sacrament is a wonderful gift of God to his children—the gift of himself to unworthy sinners:

> Thou, O Lord, my God, True God and man art wholly contained in a little likeness of Bread and Wine.[21]

> Rejoice, O my soul, and give thanks unto God for so noble a gift and so precious a comfort.[22]

We cannot really understand the Sacrament, says the *Imitation*. We can only come, to receive it in humility and reverence, to experience its value and power.

In the sacrament, God gives himself to us. But an important part of the Communion is also the offering of *ourselves* to him. We give him all our sin and transgression, to be forgiven and cleansed away. We give him all our good deeds, though they are few and imperfect, that he may sanctify them. We offer him the intercessions of all who love us and have asked us to pray for them. We offer our prayers for all who have in any way offended us, and for all those against whom we have sinned in any way, that he may forgive us all together, and remove whatever is evil from our hearts.

To receive the Sacrament worthily, we must be rightly prepared. "For every one that loveth prepareth for his beloved the best and fairest place, for thus he showeth the measure of his affection." [23] We must repent and turn away from every sin. Yet, we cannot do this by ourselves. Only his grace can make us ready—"as if a beggar were invited to sup with a rich man, and could make no return other than that of humble thanks and gratitude." [24]

With such an attitude we are not even to try to understand the mystery of the Sacrament, but simply receive it with a humble trusting heart:

> Go forward, therefore, with simple and undoubting faith, and, with the reverence of a suppliant, draw

near to the Holy Sacrament; and whatsoever thou art not able to understand, commit securely to Almighty God. God deceiveth thee not: he is deceived that trusteth too much to himself. God walketh with the simple, revealeth Himself to the humble, giveth understanding to the little ones. . . .

All reason and natural search ought to follow Faith, not to go before it, nor to break in upon it.[25]

The teaching of the whole *Imitation* is basic, unadorned, penetrating to the very heart of man's spiritual situation and need. For centuries now its wise counsel has helped to answer the prayer with which Book III closes: "Defend and keep my soul amidst so many perils of this corruptible life, and, Thy grace going with me, guide me in the way of peace to the land of everlasting light." [26]

Many of the briefer statements of the *Imitation* are as familiar as the words of the Bible, and as filled with proverbial wisdom. Gems such as these occur on nearly every page:

There is no true liberty save in the fear of God and a good conscience.[27]

Men pass away; but the truth of the Lord remaineth forever.[28]

I had rather feel contrition than understand the definition thereof.[29]

An humble rustic that serveth God is better than a proud philosopher who, neglecting the good life, contemplateth the courses of the stars.[30]

True peace of heart is to be had not by giving way to, but by resisting the passions.[31]

Man weigheth thine actions, but God weigheth thine intentions.[32]

It is good that at times we are called upon to bear adversities and crosses, for these oftentimes induce a man to re-enter his own heart.[33]

Gather some profit to thy soul wheresoever thou may be.[34]

He doeth much that loveth much.[35]

Is a man ever the better for being esteemed great of men? [36]

We may readily admit that if we were limited to the *Imitation* alone, it would not be a fully adequate guide for life. Undoubtedly it does not set forth clearly enough how we *come* to Christ, though it gives profound guidance as to how we are to *follow* him. Furthermore, Thomas à Kempis wrote as a monk for monks, and some of his statements do not apply outside the monastery. But having admitted these limitations, no thoughtful reader can escape the force of the *Imitation's* key teachings. The essence of the life in Christ is here pointedly delineated over and over again: the full surrender of ourselves to God, a keen obedience to conscience, the reverent study of the Scriptures, the cultivation of humility and brotherly love toward all men, the necessity of cross-bearing and of a deep and continuous life of prayer. Through *The Imitation of Christ* Gerhard de Groote and the Brethren of the Common Life have for more than 500 years become the teachers of the whole Christian world. Outside the Bible it is probably the world's most read Christian book.

THE SETTING: 16th-century Germany

THE BOOK: A vigorous proclamation of the believer's liberty in Christ

The Freedom of the Christian
Martin Luther

> *As our heavenly Father has in Christ freely come to our aid, we also ought freely to help our neighbor . . . and each one should become as it were a Christ to the other . . . that we may be truly Christians.*

"Out of the strong came something sweet," says an Old Testament riddle based on Samson's experience of finding honey in the body of a dead lion. Power and peaceableness are not incompatible; both are common traits of God's great men. Thus David, the man of war, also wrote the beautiful Twenty-third Psalm about green pastures and still waters. Our Lord, whose threatening words of rebuke drove the traffickers from the temple, also gently took little children in his arms and blessed them.

Martin Luther, whose life marked the transition to the modern period of church history, was a man of war in the spiritual sphere. His whole mature life was filled with controversy and struggle for the purification and renewal of the church. Luther's spirit and his fearlessness in the face of enemies are mirrored in the lines of his great Reformation Hymn:

> And though this world, with devils filled,
> Should threaten to undo us;

We will not fear, for God hath willed
His truth to triumph through us.

Yet it was this same Martin Luther who in the year 1520, in the midst of his conflict with the papacy, wrote the beautiful devotional tract, *The Freedom of the Christian Man* or *Christian Liberty*. There he set forth, with simplicity and clarity, the essence of Christian faith and life. True, even this treatise is not wholly without its controversial element, but this is minimal; the basic argument is concerned with the soul's life with God, what it is, how it is achieved, and how it expresses itself in outward life and conduct. The book is dedicated to Pope Leo X, whom Luther calls "a lamb in the midst of wolves" and "a Daniel among lions" because of the evil forces by which the Pope was surrounded. And though Luther wrote in a humble spirit, he was well aware that he had produced a truly great writing. In his letter to the Pope he says:

> It is a small book if you regard its size. Unless I am mistaken, however, it contains the whole of Christian life in a brief form, provided you grasp its meaning. I am a poor man and have no other gift to offer, and you do not need to be enriched by any but a spiritual gift.[1]

The judgment of subsequent generations has confirmed Luther's evaluation of the work.

Luther was born in 1483 in Eisleben, Germany, the son of a miner. The outward course of his life is readily charted by dates and events of significance: 1505, his entering the Augustinian monastery at Erfurt; 1508, his appointment as professor of theology at the University of Wittenberg; 1517, his nailing the 95 Theses to the door of the Castle Church; 1521, his historic trial and defense at Worms; 1522, his translation of the New Testament into German (the whole Bible in 1534); 1526, his marriage to Katherina von Bora, a former nun; 1530, the Augsburg Confession (the chief Lutheran creedal statement); 1546, his death at Eisleben.

But the truly great event in Luther's life, an event for which it is difficult to give an exact date, was his breakthrough into personal faith and freedom in Christ. We know that this came to him through his study and teaching of the Scriptures; we know that it came after many years of struggling to find peace with God through his own efforts, prayers, mortifications; we know that he was greatly helped in his quest by the words of his "spiritual father," Johannes von Staupitz, the head of his monastery. But at just what moment or in what circumstance Luther found abiding peace, scholars are not agreed. The important thing is that he did find the way; the light did dawn; wonderful liberation in and through the Word of God *did* come to him. It is of this that he writes, so earnestly and so fervently, to Pope Leo in *The Freedom of the Christian.*

Luther begins by summarizing the main argument of his treatise in a double statement, now familiar and oft-quoted: "A Christian is a perfectly free lord of all, and subject to none. A Christian is a perfectly dutiful servant of all, and subject to all." [2] This statement indicates the two main parts of the treatise, in the first of which Luther shows how the inner man is set free by faith alone; and in the second of which he shows that, nevertheless, works are a necessary part of the outward man's existence. We live by faith, but faith necessarily issues in Christian works. A true Christian life must include both. Says Luther:

> Man has a twofold nature, a spiritual and a bodily one. According to the spiritual nature, which men refer to as the soul, he is called a spiritual, inner, or new man. According to the bodily nature, which men refer to as the flesh, he is called a carnal, outward or old man. . . . Because of this diversity of nature the Scriptures assert contradictory things concerning the same man, since these two men in the same man contradict each other.[3]

The inner man, Luther says, cannot be profited or helped by outward acts, such as eating and drinking, wearing sacred vestments, living in holy places, going on pilgrimages, fasting, and similar activities, "Such works produce nothing but hypocrites." [4] What the soul really needs, and the *only* thing that it needs absolutely is the Word of God—that is, the gospel concerning Christ, incarnate, suffering, risen, and glorified. Only by receiving this gospel can the soul be saved; and true preaching is to set forth this gospel in such a way that men may lay hold upon it in faith. "With the heart man believes unto righteousness," and by no outward labor of any kind can the inward man be justified, made free, and saved.

The Scriptures are made up of *precepts* and *promises,* law and gospel. The precepts teach what is good and what ought to be done, but they give no power to do it. It is when the law has convicted a man of his wrongdoing and humbled him, that the gospel, the promises of God, granted by faith can set him free.

> That which is impossible for you to accomplish by trying to fulfill all the works of the law—many and useless as they all are—you will accomplish quickly and easily through faith. God our Father has made all things depend on faith so that whoever has faith will have everything, and whoever does not have faith will have nothing. . . . If a touch of Christ healed, how much more will this tender spiritual touch, this absorbing of the Word, communicate to the soul all things that belong to the Word. This, then, is how through faith alone without works the soul is justified by the Word of God, sanctified, made true, peaceful, and free, filled with every blessing and truly made a child of God.[5]

Faith has such great power, says Luther, for three reasons: First, it is *in* the soul. It is not merely an external activity which may not reach the heart of man at all. Just as iron exposed to fire glows because of the fire, so the believing soul is made to "glow" with life because of the indwelling Word. Second, faith alone truly honors God; in fact, it gives him the highest honor possible, because it holds him to be truthful and worthy of trust. What higher credit can we attribute to anyone than truth and absolute goodness? Thus the soul cleaves to the promises of God, deeming him absolutely trustworthy. Third, faith unites the soul to Christ as a wife to her husband, by which mystery, as the Apostle teaches, Christ and the soul are made "one flesh." Human marriages are but feeble types of this one great marriage.

> Christ is full of grace, life, and salvation; the soul is full of sin, death, and damnation. Now let faith come between them and sins, death, and damnation will be Christ's while grace, life, and salvation will be the soul's.

All this takes place, says Luther, through "the wedding ring of faith." "Who can comprehend the riches of the glory of this grace? Here this rich and divine bridegroom Christ marries this poor, wicked harlot, redeems her from all her evil and adorns her with all His goodness!" [6]

Through faith alone we too become kings and priests to God, like Christ our soul's husband. All things are subject to him, as King and High Priest, and he both intercedes for us and teaches us inwardly through his Spirit. And these great privileges he communicates also to every believer: all who believe in Christ are kings and priests in him. As to kingship, the believer is exalted above all things in spiritual power, so that all are subject to him—for "strength is made perfect in weakness," and the soul can turn all things to the profit of its salvation. And as priests we are called to appear before God and pray for others, and to teach one another mutually the things that are of God. The "priesthood" does not belong to a few selected individuals, called priests or ministers, but to all believers—even though all are not called to teach or preach publicly.

Those who are called to preach, however, must truly *preach Christ,* that is, not only preach *about* Christ in a historical manner, but proclaim him in such a way that faith is created in the hearts of the hearers, so "that He may not only be Christ but a Christ for you and for me. . . . Such faith is produced and preserved in us by preaching why Christ came, what He brought and bestowed, what benefit it is to us to accept Him." [7] To be a preacher of the gospel is indeed a high, sometimes almost an overwhelming, calling.

In his discussion of the outward man, Luther is very emphatic that he does not underrate the value of good works. Good works are an essential and important part of the Christian life, even though they can contribute nothing to our salvation. We are saved by faith alone—to repeat his figure, by being "married to Christ." But when we have been saved by faith, good works are a natural and inevitable consequence. Good works serve especially two important purposes: first, to discipline the body, because we are still living in the world with its temptations and enticements; and secondly, to serve our neighbor, who is also in the world. Good works do not make us good—just as a good house does not make a good builder, but a good builder makes a good house. Or in the words of Christ, "a good tree cannot bear evil fruit, neither can a bad tree bear good fruit" (Matt. 7:18). Works can never justify us before God. But our good works can show our *gratitude* to God. Good works are done freely, gratuitously. And therefore they can be truly effective also in behalf of our neighbor. The Christian lives not for himself, but for others. And he does this freely—"in the freest servitude." Thus he also follows the example of Christ, his Lord. Christ gave up his all for us, and took the form of a servant. So should we also do for others.

> Although the Christian is thus free from all works, he ought in this liberty to empty himself, take upon himself the form of a servant, be made in the likeness of men, . . . serve, help, and in every way deal with his neighbor as he sees that God through Christ has dealt and still deals with him.[8]

Luther even goes on to say, regarding the Christian's works:

> I will therefore give myself as a Christ to my neighbor, just as Christ offered himself to me; I will do

nothing in this life except what I see is necessary, profitable, and salutary to my neighbor, since through faith I have an abundance of all good things in Christ.[9]

The good things we have from God should flow from one to the other and be common to all, so that every one should "put on" his neighbor and so conduct himself toward him as if he himself were in the other's place. . . . I should lay before God my faith and my righteousness that they may cover and intercede for the sins of my neighbor which I take upon myself and so labor and serve in them as if they were my very own. That is what Christ did for us. . . .

We conclude, therefore, that a Christian lives not in himself, but in Christ and in his neighbor. Otherwise he is not a Christian. He lives in Christ through faith, in his neighbor through love. By faith he is caught up beyond himself into God. By love he descends beneath himself into his neighbor. Yet he always remains in God and in his love.[10]

The end of Christian faith is not only the salvation of the individual soul, but rather the building of true Christian community. Luther had a great vision of the Kingdom—the city of the Living God, coming down from God out of heaven. Because of the way the gospel had been perverted and misrepresented, he seemed at times to be condemning good works of kingdom-building. But his concern was simply to put the gospel as proclaimed in the New Testament into crystal-clear perspective. In *The Freedom of the Christian,* he outlines the basis for a truly spiritual devotional life: a living faith constantly flowering forth in Christlike loving service building the communion of saints. To see this vision of faith and works, gospel and law, in true perspective, is indeed to know the reality of Christian freedom.

THE SETTING: 16th-century Spain

THE BOOK: St. Teresa's portrayal of the "seven mansions" of the soul's spiritual growth

The Interior Castle
St. Teresa of Avila

When the silkworm is full-grown, it starts to spin its silk and to build the house in which it is to die.

The sixteenth century was in many respects the greatest century in the history of Spain. It was the age of exploration and swiftly expanding national power. The foundations were laid for far-flung Spanish rule in the New World, and in Europe Spain challenged the might of England reaching toward its height under Elizabeth I. It was also the Golden Age of Spanish literature, the time of Cervantes, Lope de Vega, and a little later Calderón. But, equally important with political and literary advance, sixteenth-century Spain was marked by a remarkable flowering of the spiritual life, expressing itself in saintly lives, in a stream of notable spiritual books, and in vigorous reform movements in the church. Many of the greatest names of Spanish spirituality belong to this period: Teresa of Avila, John of the Cross, Luis of Granada, Ignatius Loyola, and many more. Among them the name of St. Teresa shines most brightly of all, not only because of the profundity of her thought, but because her message, while truly mystical, is geared to the level of the

55

common reader. In the works of St. Teresa, Spanish religious writing comes to us in its most attractive and beloved form.

As St. Teresa begins *The Interior Castle,* she tells how the idea for the book first came to her in answer to prayer: it was to picture the human soul as a beautiful castle with many rooms, and to describe the methods whereby the soul "enters into itself" in its quest for a deepening life of fellowship with God.

> While I was beseeching the Lord today that He would speak through me . . . I began to think of the soul as if it were a castle made of a single diamond or of very clear crystal, in which there are many rooms, just as in heaven there are many mansions.[1]

A little further on she continues,

> Now let us return to our beautiful and delightful castle and see how we can enter it. I seem rather to be talking nonsense, . . . For we ourselves are the castle; and it would be absurd to tell someone to enter a room where he was in it already! But you must understand that there are many ways of "being" in a place. Many souls remain in the outer court of the castle, . . . and have no idea what there is in that wonderful place, or who dwells in it, or even how many rooms it has. You will have read certain books on prayer which advise the soul to enter within itself: and that is exactly what this means. . . . As far as I can understand, the door of entry into this castle is prayer and meditation.[2]

The Interior Castle was written during a period of about six months in the year 1577, as a spiritual guide for a group of nuns who were St. Teresa's "disciples." But very soon after its publication it became widely known as a work of great spiritual wisdom not only for the religious (there were hundreds of monasteries and convents in Spain in St. Teresa's day), but for untold numbers of lay people as well. Steadily it was spread by republication and translation into many languages, and now for centuries it has been treasured throughout the world as one of the great classics of the spiritual life. Few books give as keen and detailed an analysis of Christian experience, from the time of the soul's awakening, through all its struggles, defeats, and victories, until it reaches the very portals of heaven.

Teresa was born in Avila, in central Spain, in 1515. The daughter of well-to-do and noble parents, a girl of romantic and ardent temperament, fond of pleasure and social life, Teresa nevertheless early felt the drawing of God upon her heart. Before she was 20, she entered a Carmelite convent. But she was not really happy there. Her heart was not at peace. A long and severe illness, during which she was paralyzed for about two years, seemed only to lead to further relaxation of her life and interests. A period of deep inward struggle followed, lasting for years. In her autobiography she writes of that time:

> On the one hand God was calling me. On the other, I was following the world. All the things of God gave me pleasure, yet I was tied and bound to those of the world. It seemed as if I wanted to reconcile these two contradictory things, . . . —the life of the spirit and the pleasures and joys and pastimes of the senses. . . . I spent nearly twenty years on that stormy sea, often falling in this way and each time rising again, but to little purpose, as I would only fall once more.[3]

Not until she was in her forty-first year did the conflict cease. Then one day as she was praying before the statue of Christ being scourged, a new peace came to her, and a new and deeper life of prayer. Visions came too, and voices and seasons of rapturous ecstasy. It was for her the beginning of a continuing mystical experience. In her own analysis of these experiences, however, she always minimized any emphasis on visions or ecstatic states. For her, what mattered most was always the soul's surrender to God and walk with him, in humility and faith.

Teresa's experiences with God in her own life led her to be

impatient with the spiritual laxity that prevailed in the convents of her order. She was convinced that without discipline,
the spiritual life is sure to suffer. So during the latter part of
her life, Teresa led a far-reaching movement for reform in the
Carmelite Order. She put into force again many of the order's
original principles and practices. Her followers and the convents
she founded and led, sixteen in number, were called the Car-
melites of the Discalced and Primitive Order. In this effort to
reform she often encountered bitter opposition and persecution.
But she prevailed. Whether the specific practices she advocated
(for example, going barefoot) would be approved today, is less
important than the *spirit* she exemplified and sought to impart.
This spirit is expressed powerfully and beautifully—for Teresa
is among the great prose writers of Spain of any age—in her
four great books, *The Way of Perfection, The Book of Foundations,* the *Life,* and *The Interior Castle.* This last was written only a few years before her death and embodied her mature
thought in the most ordered form. Of this book Evelyn Underhill says: "It is full of Teresa's own bracing spirit; her dislike of
all pretensions, all seeking for consolations, all idle and dreamy
enjoyments, all spiritual conceit." [4] It is one of the world's
masterpieces of spirituality.

One of the most remarkable things about Teresa of Avila was
her combination of the highest degree of inward spiritual experience with the greatest practical ability in dealing with human
affairs. Prayer and administration were alike her forte and her
pleasure. "She could turn from directions about the finances of
the community or the right sweeping down of the house, to deal
in a manner equally wise and precise with the most delicate
problems of the soul." [5] Her books, filled with spiritual wisdom,
were written in the intervals in her administrative work and
her tiring journeys as a founder and reformer of religious houses.
She herself was a remarkable combination of Mary and Martha,
a combination she urgently recommended to her followers in her
description of the Seventh Mansion.

The Interior Castle, or as it is commonly called in the Spanish
editions, *The Mansions,* remains St. Teresa's greatest book, both

because of its finished form, and because of its depth in spiritual understanding. The basic symbolism of the "castle made up of a single diamond, having many rooms" permits the author to deal with the problems of the spiritual life at every level, from the soul's first trembling response to the voice of God, to the highest reaches of prayer and contemplation.

Before considering some of the teachings of *The Interior Castle,* it is important to recall that it was written for the instruction of a group of nuns who were already members of the convent community. St. Teresa, with her long experience and keen insight into human psychology and spirituality, knew well that many who had entered the "religious" life had really only taken the first steps along the way of Christ. There were many "mansions" for them yet to traverse in their quest of Christlike perfection. St. Teresa is surely right when she urges them not to be content to be merely "within the castle walls."

St. Teresa's analysis and portrayal of the various stages of spiritual development may at times seem to be somewhat mechanical or overdone. But we may be sure that she did not intend them to be interpreted too literally or legalistically. We might say that the stages described are meant to be *suggestive,* not *normative.*

In the First Mansion we are given a vivid picture of the state of the soul at the beginning of its pilgrimage:

> The soul is still absorbed in worldly affairs . . . and puffed up by worldly honors and ambitions. There are so many bad things—snakes and vipers and poisonous creatures—which have come in with the soul that they prevent it from seeing the light. . . . These wild beasts and animals force him to close his eyes to everything but themselves.[6]

In the Second Mansion, the soul has begun to practice prayer, but not with full diligence, and it has not learned to avoid occasions of sin, "which is a very perilous condition." But God is continuing to call these souls, and, says St. Teresa:

> As they gradually get nearer to the place where His
> Majesty dwells, He becomes a very good Neighbor
> to them. And even when we are engaged in worldly
> pastimes and businesses and pleasures and hagglings,
> when we are falling into sins and rising from them
> again—in spite of all that . . . He calls us ceaselessly,
> time after time, to approach Him . . .
>
> His appeals come through the conversations of good
> people, or from sermons, or through the reading of
> good books. . . . Or they come through sicknesses and
> trials, or by means of truth which God teaches us at
> times when we are engaged in prayer.[7]

The Third Mansion portrays the soul struggling with minor
ethical problems, still not finding great joy or freedom in prayer.
In the Fourth Mansion, however, it begins to attain to a definitely higher level of prayer—prayer less dependent on its own
efforts and activities and more on the indwelling work of God's
Spirit in the heart. To make clear the meaning of this higher
type of prayer, St. Teresa makes use of a helpful illustration:

> To understand it [the prayer of quiet] better, let us
> suppose that we are looking at two fountains the
> basins of which can be filled with water. . . . These
> two large basins can be filled with water in different
> ways: the water in the one comes from a long dis-
> tance, by means of numerous conduits and through
> human skill; but the other has been constructed at
> the very source of the water and fills without making
> any noise.[8]

The water from the first of these fountains, explains St. Teresa,
"corresponds to the spiritual sweetness which is produced by
meditation" (in other words, by our own spiritual efforts). To
the second fountain the water comes direct from its source, which
is God, and when "He is pleased to grant us some supernatural
favor, its coming is accompanied by the greatest peace and quietness and sweetness within ourselves." [9]

In other words, St. Teresa teaches that there is a higher level of prayer where, as it were, not we but the Spirit of God speaks in our hearts. This is in harmony with Paul's teaching in Romans 8, but perhaps all too few Christians enter into this experience. St. Teresa reminds us that this too is a gift, not a human achievement. "However many tears we shed, we cannot produce this water in those ways; it is given only to whom God wills to give it and often when the soul is not thinking of it at all." [10]

Going a step further, in the Fifth Mansion, in her most famous metaphor St. Teresa likens the soul to an ugly crawling silkworm which is enabled to build a cocoon where it is to die, and which then comes forth as a beautiful soaring white butterfly. By the transforming power of the Holy Spirit it has been purified and set free into a wondrous new life with God.

> It sets no store by the things it did when it was a worm. . . . It has wings now: how can it be content to crawl along slowly when it is able to fly? All that it can do for God seems to it slight by comparison with its desires.[11]

The soul has found a new life of liberty, but it is still far from its goal. There are struggles and temptations yet to be overcome—some gross and horrid, others subtle and difficult to detect —before it finally reaches fullness of peace.

But the Spirit ever leads on, guiding, warning, strengthening, encouraging. In the Sixth Mansion the soul's faith and love are more stabilized. Prayer has become very precious, and it finds its joy in doing the will of God, no matter how difficult. But it also endures new trials. Often it is misunderstood even by close associates, who doubt its sincerity. "How holy she's getting!" they exclaim.[12] Nevertheless it presses on, calmly, bravely, and at last—sometimes after years (there are *eleven* chapters in the Sixth Mansion!)—it attains to the beatitude of the Seventh Mansion.

Now the soul is at peace. It has entered into the Spiritual Marriage, the life of union with God. Storms and temptations may rage around it, but peace abides within—the peace that passes all understanding. Concerning the new levels of prayer experienced in this blessed state St. Teresa writes:

> The Lord appears in the center of the soul . . . just
> as He appeared to the Apostles, without entering
> through the door, when he said to them, 'Pax vobis!'
> This instantaneous communication of God to the soul
> is so great a secret and so sublime a favor, and such
> delight is felt by the soul, that I do not know with
> what to compare it, beyond saying that the Lord is
> pleased to manifest to the soul at that moment the
> glory that is in Heaven, in a more sublime manner
> than is possible through any vision or spiritual consolation.[13]

But even here the soul must cling to God if it is to be kept secure. St. Teresa makes it clear that she does not teach "sinless perfection." As long as the soul is in the world, it is not beyond the possibility of temptation and sin.

> I may seem to be giving the impression that, when
> the soul reaches the state in which God grants it this
> favor, it is sure of its salvation and free from the risk
> of backsliding. But that is not my meaning.[14]

The times of trial and suffering are not past; yet peace reigns within. So complete is this peace of God which guards the heart that even opposition and persecution only serve to deepen it.

> When these souls are persecuted again, they have a
> great interior joy. . . . They bear no enmity with those
> who ill-treat them, or desire to do so. Indeed they conceive a special love for them.[15]

The ideal of Christian sanctification portrayed in these quotations is so exalted that we are tempted to ask: "Who is sufficient for these things?" St. Teresa knows well that by no means all Christians will attain to the peace and victory of the Seventh Mansion. But she also knows the secret of such prevailing spiritual victory: it is the vision and companionship of Christ.

Fix your eyes on the Crucified and nothing else will be of much importance to you. . . . Do you know when people really become spiritual? It is when they become slaves of God and are branded with his sign, which is the sign of the Cross, in token that they have given Him their freedom. Then He can sell them as slaves to the whole world, as He Himself was sold.[16]

Through the teachings of *The Interior Castle* we are led into the deepest valleys and to the highest summits of spiritual experience. As we read we marvel at both the purity of the author's spirit and the sublimity of her words. Much of the time, especially in the later Mansions, she seems far beyond us. But when we falter or grow discouraged, it is good to know that also she lived by an utterly simple faith, expressed in her beautiful and oft-quoted poem:

Let nothing disturb thee,
Nothing affright thee;
All things are passing;
God never changeth;
Patient endurance
Attaineth to all things;
Who God possesseth
In nothing is wanting;
Alone God sufficeth.[17]

THE SETTING: 16th- and 17th-century England

THE BOOK: The time-tested manual of prayer and worship of the Anglican Church

The Book of Common Prayer

. . . that all who profess and call themselves Christians may be led into the way of truth, and hold the faith in unity of spirit, in the bond of peace, and in righteousness of life.

No other devotional book has so molded the religious life of a whole nation as has the *Book of Common Prayer* of the Church of England. Its influence, both religious and literary, has been second only to that of the King James Bible. Since the Church of England is "established," its official forms of public prayer and worship are prescribed by law. Thus the forms and words of the *Book of Common Prayer* become familiar from childhood to the great majority of the English people. But its world-wide use is by no means due only to prescription. Through more than four centuries the Prayer Book has become precious to a host of readers and users, not only in the Anglican (Episcopal) churches throughout the world, but among many of the other Protestant denominations as well. Among Roman Catholics too the Prayer Book has many lovers, partly because it is largely derived from medieval worship forms. And it has been translated, in whole or in part, into more than 150 languages or dialects.

The Prayer Book has been slightly modified in the various Anglican churches, but these changes are minor. The American Prayer Book, adopted in 1789, reflects the political changes which had come with independence, but also states clearly that "this church is far from intending to depart from the Church of England in any essential point of doctrine, discipline or worship." [1] The same would be true of the other Anglican Prayer Book versions in other countries. Throughout the world, the Prayer Book remains both a bulwark of the faith and a treasured guide for the spiritual life. Bishop Robert E. L. Strider has well expressed the high esteem in which it is held:

> To those who know and love it, the Prayer Book is not only a precious heritage from the Christian ages, enshrining in terms of lovely human speech the best men have thought about God, freedom and human destiny, but it is also a practical manual of worship public and private and a well-tested guide to all who would know and serve God more truly. . . . It makes ever fresh appeal to generations of Churchmen as they come and go. [2]

The first edition of the *Book of Common Prayer*, largely the work of Archbishop Thomas Cranmer, was published in 1549 in the reign of King Edward VI. Subsequently there were several other editions, with minor amendments, yielding to strong Catholic pressure under Queen Mary I, returning to more Protestant forms under Queen Elizabeth I, and reflecting a slight Puritan influence from the Commonwealth period. The form finally approved in 1662 has remained essentially unchanged, though various larger and smaller revisions have frequently been proposed.

Archbishop Cranmer wanted to give to his people, in their own language, and in one not-too-large volume, the chief liturgical treasures of the medieval church—purged from those teachings which had gradually grown up through the centuries but had no true basis in Scripture. Concerning Cranmer's high achievement, Percy Dearmer, an Anglican scholar, has said:

Cranmer stands apart. . . . He was able to bring his own great gift to the Reformation—a power of liturgical art which places him among the great prose writers of the world. Others worked with him and after him, as others had worked before, and the beauty of their united product is a witness to the greatness of that age of literature which covered the hundred years between the first Prayer Book and the last, and gave us Shakespeare, Bacon, and Milton . . . and the Authorized Version of the Bible.[3]

The Prayer Book maintains a style that is always clear and beautiful, often noble and sublime. While at times its 16th-century language may impress us as having a slightly old-fashioned flavor, like the Authorized Version of the Bible, only seldom does this interfere with our understanding, and often it adds to the spiritual impact.

The literary qualities of the Prayer Book are, however, not the most important. The most basic reason for its worldwide and enduring appeal is unquestionably its thoroughly *biblical* character. From beginning to end, in both thought and language, it is based upon Scripture. In fact, approximately two-thirds consists of actual quotations from the Bible. And the remaining materials, the prayers, the orders of worship, the occasional services, even the creeds and catechism—are cast largely in Scriptural wording. It could almost be said that the Prayer Book is the Bible arranged and paraphrased for devotional use.

Closely related to the biblical character of the Prayer Book is the fact that it is *churchly* in its whole spirit and orientation. Its authors, rather than simply devising new forms, drew freely upon more than fifteen hundred years of the worship experience of the church. The result is a work of profound, tested spiritual substance. The devotional life which it recommends is not of any individualistic sort. It is the book of *common* prayer. Its major services of prayer are intended to be conducted when the people of God are assembled in his house. Both the festival and the occasional services presuppose the leadership of an ordained minister. This does not preclude a large participation by the laity, both in the reading of the Scriptures and in prayer and song. Nor does it make unnecessary other, wholly informal meetings. The point is rather that the basic devotional pattern of the Prayer Book is definitely church-oriented. The Christian is to find his way forward, and homeward, not alone but among the people of God.

Finally, we may mention as a reason for the universal appeal of the *Book of Common Prayer* its comprehensive character. It provides forms and patterns of worship for many diverse occasions and needs: the public worship service; the administration of the sacraments; the "landmark occasions" of birth, baptism, confirmation, marriage, death, burial; family prayers; the ordination of pastors and the consecration of bishops. There are prayers for the dying, and an order for anointing in illness. And the Book certainly finds much of its usefulness in the believer's private devotions, though it was not written with this as a chief purpose. It is a book for all seasons, and for all Christians.

Not all Christians, however, will find it immediately appealing and devotionally satisfying. In both style and content it is more conservative than contemporary. To follow its guidance is basically not an emotional experience. It is rather like coming into a great cathedral where solemn music is being played, or like experiencing a true friendship, which ripens with the years.

As to the relative appeal of the various parts of the Prayer Book, there are differences of taste and preference, but universally beloved have been the hundreds of prayers and collects which occur throughout the volume. Some are parts of worship services; many are designated for a certain Sunday or feast day; others stand alone, usually with titles indicating their appropriate use. There are prayers suited to almost every occasion and circumstance in life, each reflecting some aspect of the soul's quest of God and life with him.

Among the many examples that might be given of especially inspiring prayers, here are some of the best known and loved:

A Collect for Grace

O Lord, our heavenly Father, Almighty and everlasting God, who hast safely brought us to the beginning of this day; defend us in the same with thy mighty power; and grant that this day we fall into no sin, neither run into any kind of danger; but that all our doings, being ordered by thy governance, may be righteous in thy sight; through Jesus Christ our Lord. Amen.[4]

The General Thanksgiving

Almighty God, Father of all mercies, we, thine unworthy servants, do give thee most humble and hearty thanks for all thy goodness and loving-kindness to us, and to all men. We bless thee for our creation, preservation, and all the blessings of this life; but above all, for thine inestimable love in the redemption of the world by our Lord Jesus Christ; for the means of grace, and for the hope of glory. And, we beseech thee, give us that due sense of all thy mercies, that our hearts may be unfeignedly thankful; and that we show forth thy praise, not only with our lips, but in our lives, by giving up our selves to thy service, and by walking before thee in holiness and righteousness all our days; through Jesus Christ our Lord, to whom, with thee and the Holy Ghost, be all honour and glory, world without end. Amen.[5]

The Collect for the Second Sunday in Advent

Blessed Lord, who hast caused all holy Scriptures to be written for our learning; Grant that we may in such wise hear them, read, mark, learn, and inwardly digest them, that by patience and comfort of thy holy Word, we may embrace, and ever hold fast, the blessed hope of everlasting life, which thou hast given us in our Saviour Jesus Christ. Amen.[6]

For Guidance

O God, by whom the meek are guided in judgment, and light riseth up in darkness for the godly; Grant us, in all our doubts and uncertainties, the grace to ask what thou wouldst have us to do, that the Spirit of Wisdom may save us from all false choices, and that in thy light we may see light, and in thy straight path may not stumble; through Jesus Christ our Lord. Amen.[7]

At Night

O Lord, support us all the day long, until the shadows lengthen and the evening comes, and the busy world is hushed, and the fever of life is over, and our work is done. Then in thy mercy grant us a safe lodging, and a holy rest, and peace at the last. Amen.[8]

Sometimes the question is raised: is it really a healthy practice to use set forms of prayer? Is it not better that all our prayers be spontaneous, arising directly out of the needs of our own hearts? Surely *much* of our prayer should be in our own words; but the long experience of Christians tells us that there is room and need for both types. To quote Percy Dearmer again:

There is some loss in the use of printed words, but there is greater gain. We have in them the accumulated wisdom and beauty of the Christian Church, the garnered excellence of many saints. We are by them released from the accidents of time and place. Above all we are preserved against the worst dangers of selfishness: in the common prayer we join together in a great fellowship that is as wide as the world; and we are guided, not by the limited notions of our own minister, nor by the narrow impulses of our own desires, but by the mighty voice that rises from the general heart of Christendom.[9]

Much of the *Book of Common Prayer* is taken up with forms for public worship, and these too are beautiful, thought-stirring, and edifying. For many of us they will differ considerably from the forms to which we are most accustomed, but even when this is so, a common note of humility, awe, thanksgiving, and petition pervades all the forms of true worship, including these. The liturgies contained in the *Book of Common Prayer* are, as we have noted, largely rooted in the worship practices of past centuries. Praying these "common prayers" even the most unconventional and informal of Christians scarcely fail to experience as did the psalmist of old that *"strength* and *beauty* are in thy sanctuary."

One of the very useful parts of the *Book of Common Prayer,* which might easily be overlooked, is the division of the Psalter into readings for morning and evening prayer for each day of a month. The Psalms never wear out. The monks used to chant the whole Psalter every week. The *Book of Common Prayer* makes the task easier for us by distributing it over a whole month. The Prayer Book version of the Psalms differs somewhat from the King James, but in most instances this only adds to the reader's interest.

The appointed Epistle and Gospel readings, arranged for all the Sundays and Holy Days, a very important section making up more than one-fourth of the entire Prayer Book, gather up the treasured usages of ages past, and following the worship pattern of the church year, provide an ever-renewed source of grace and spiritual enrichment. The texts are those generally followed in the liturgical churches. A complete table of daily Scripture readings is also provided, covering practically the entire Bible in a year, with some of the greatest passages read at least twice. The *Book of Common Prayer* is indeed a guide and companion into all the Scriptures and along every way of life.

In the church of Christ, there is "one Body and one Spirit, one Lord, one faith, one baptism, one God and Father of all." But there are still many divisions and denominations. Christ still prays: "That they all may be one." Ecumenism is still a largely unattained goal, though now that goal seems to be com-

ing nearer. As through the *Book of Common Prayer* we gratefully receive from the riches one of the great traditions of
Christendom, and look forward to the ever fuller realization of
"one Body and one Spirit," we may fittingly pray, in Prayer
Book words:

> O God, who hast made of one blood all nations of
> men for to dwell on the face of the whole earth, and
> didst send thy blessed Son to preach peace to them
> that are far off and to them that are nigh; Grant that
> all men everywhere may seek after thee and find thee.
> Bring the nations into thy fold, pour out thy Spirit
> upon all flesh, and hasten thy kingdom; through the
> same thy Son Jesus Christ our Lord. Amen.[10]

THE SETTING: 17th-century France

THE BOOK: A humble kitchen worker shares the secret of unbroken fellowship with God

The Practice of the Presence of God

Brother Lawrence

The time of business does not with me differ from the time of prayer.

In the fields of both science and religion the great forward steps have usually been the result of a new, sometimes startling, insight into a previously unknown truth. Often this is expressed in a *simplified* statement of that truth. That the earth and other planets revolve about the sun, that lightning is a form of electricity, that some substances are radioactive: these are all truths that became known through epoch-making scientific discovery. In the field of science such insights have usually come as a result of great learning. The discoverers were men of wide knowledge and keen intellect, sometimes of genius.

In the field of religion, however, while many of the great pioneers were persons of both outstanding talent and thorough education, often this was not so. Moses was, it is true, trained in the learning of the Egyptians and Isaiah lived at court, but Amos and Micah were men from the countryside. Paul was well-educated, but Peter and several of the other Apostles were fishermen. George Fox was an unschooled tailor; D. L. Moody was a shoe-clerk; Richard Allen, the founder and leader of one of the great American denominations, was a former slave who had purchased his own freedom.

Among the host of these unlettered prophets who have enriched the life of the church through important spiritual insight or leadership, one of the most unforgettable figures is that of the Carmelite lay brother Nicholas Herman, best known by his monastic name, Brother Lawrence. Brother Lawrence's teachings concerning the practice of the presence of God strike a keynote which has made him the unobtrusive but exceedingly effective teacher of many generations of Christians.

It would be hard to imagine a life course less promising than that of Brother Lawrence: born and reared in poverty, receiving only the most meager education, serving as a soldier and a household servant; finally, dissatisfied with what life had had to offer, entering a monastery and being assigned to the most menial duties in the kitchen. Yet in that humble setting he steadily "grew in favor with God and men," so that in his later years he was sought out for his spiritual counsel by many of the prominent churchmen of Paris. After his death a friend, who was vicar to one of the Parisian prelates, was authorized to publish notes from some of Brother Lawrence's conversations, adding to them also a number of his letters. Together they form only a slender volume, but within its few pages are distilled precious lessons concerning the heart of the spiritual life. In the 300 years since Brother Lawrence's death, the book has been reprinted again and again, translated into many languages, and, prized alike by Catholics and Protestants, it has been circulated throughout the world. Perhaps a chief secret of its popularity is the unadorned beauty of Brother Lawrence's own life which clearly shines through its simple pages. The preface to a current edition gives this characterization of the author:

> A wholly consecrated man, he lived his life as if he were a singing pilgrim on the march, as happy in serving his fellow monks and brothers from the monastery kitchen as in serving God in the vigil of prayer and

penance. He died at eighty years of age, full of love
and years and honored by all who knew him, leaving
a name which has been as "precious ointment poured
forth." [1]

Born in 1611 in Lorraine, France, Nicholas Herman was already past middle life when he joined the barefooted Carmel-
ites and was assigned to his kitchen duties. Those duties were
at first very distasteful to him; he was, he says, "a clumsy fellow who broke everything." Likewise, he had little taste for the
business dealings sometimes connected with his work. But he
accepted all of it as God's will for him, and gradually gained
the great insight which he later so gladly taught to others: that
God is present in even the most commonplace of circumstances.
Brother Lawrence himself spent his whole life, thenceforth, as
a "servant of the servants of God" among the pots and kettles.
He died in 1691 when he was 80.

The heart of Brother Lawrence's message, given in the very
title of his book, *The Practice of the Presence of God,* is con-
cisely stated in a passage in the first letter:

Having found in many books different methods of
going to God, and divers practices of the spiritual
life, I thought this would serve rather to puzzle me
than facilitate what I sought after, which was nothing
but how to become wholly God's. This made me re-
solve to give all for the all; so after having given myself wholly to God, that He might take away my sin,
I renounced, for the love of Him, everything that was
not He, and I began to live as if there was none but
He and I in the world. Sometimes I considered myself
before Him as a poor criminal before his judge; at
other times I beheld Him in my heart as my Father,
as my God. . . . I worshipped Him the oftenest that I
could, keeping my mind in His Holy presence, and
recalling it as often as I found it wandered from
Him. . . . I continued it . . . without troubling or

disquieting myself when my mind had wandered involuntarily. I made this my business as much all the day long as at the appointed times of prayer; for at all times, every hour, every minute, even in the height of my business, I drove away from my mind everything that was capable of interrupting my thought of God.[2]

The profound truths contained in this letter were not the result of a single simple experience, however. They grew out of a background of many years of walking with God. The beginnings of his conversion, he tells us, came when he was eighteen years of age. His account is reported in the first recorded conversation:

In the winter, seeing a tree stripped of its leaves, and considering that within a little time the leaves would be renewed, and after that the flowers and fruit appear, he received a high view of the providence and power of God, which has never since been effaced from his soul. This view had perfectly set him loose from the world and kindled in him such a love for God that he could not tell whether it had increased during the more than forty years he had lived since.[3]

He did not come to full spiritual clarity at once. Though he wanted to love and serve God, he found that the flesh was weak. For ten years, his faith was wavering and marked by inward struggle. Then suddenly he was set free.

For the first ten years, I suffered much. . . . During this time I fell often, and rose again presently. . . . When I thought of nothing but to end my days in these troubles . . . I found myself changing all at once; and my soul . . . felt a profound inward peace, as if she were in her center and place of rest.[4]

This spiritual liberation set him free, too, from any slavish devotion to religious forms. He learned to rejoice in God alone.

I have quitted all forms of devotion and set prayers but those to which my state obliges me. And I make it my business only to persevere in His holy presence, wherein I keep myself by a simple attention, and a general fond regard to God, which I may call an *actual presence* of God.[5]

And though he constantly found God in his work, Brother Lawrence's religion was by no means one of "works," but thoroughly evangelical:

All possible kinds of mortification, if they were void of the love of God, could not efface a single sin. We ought, without anxiety, to expect the pardon of our sins from the blood of Jesus Christ, only endeavoring to love him with all our hearts.[6]

Work and prayer for him became parts of one unified pattern of life.

In addition to its central and oft-reiterated emphasis on practicing the Presence, Brother Lawrence's book has a number of important subordinate teachings regarding the Christian life. One of these, seen especially in the letters, points to the singular beauty of true Christian friendship. He is concerned, chiefly, to give counsel regarding various practical problems—illness and infirmity, doubt, loneliness. But whether he writes to men or women, breathing through these letters is a spirit of warm Christ-centered friendship. One of its constant expressions is mutual intercessory prayer, simply, directly, asked for and given: "Pray to Him for me as I pray to Him for you. I hope to see Him quickly." [7]

Another strong impression made by Brother Lawrence is his complete freedom from dogmatism. His theological views are orthodox, but he does not stress them. Faith for him is a practical matter, rooted in his own experience of the grace of God, tested and proved in everyday life. He is not at all interested in winning anyone else to his theology. His book does not contain a single direct quotation of Scripture. Yet the light of Christ and the life in Christ shine through it all. This wholly indirect approach to the dogmas of religion is certainly one of the secrets of Brother Lawrence's universal appeal.

The reader cannot fail to note, too, that despite its very elementary subject matter and its complete lack of literary pretense, *The Practice of the Presence* has, scattered throughout its pages, many singularly apt phrases characterizing the spiritual life: we are to serve God "with a holy freedom"; [8] our fellowship with him is "a commerce of love"; [9] as his friends we are invited "to eat at the King's table"; [10] we are urged to enter into "the oratory of the heart"; [11] we must "give all for all"; [12] "those who have the gale of the Holy Spirit go forward even in sleep." [13] Brother Lawrence does not think abstractly, but practically, and the practice of God's presence is for him a quiet symphony of service, faith, and love.

And his vision of God, intertwining and uniting all aspects of his life, remains clear, unbroken, persistent to the end. To an elderly friend, stricken with illness, he writes in one of his last letters:

> He requires no great matters of us: . . . a little adoration; sometimes to pray for His grace, sometimes to offer Him your sufferings, and sometimes to return Him thanks for the favours He has given you, and still gives you, in the midst of your troubles. . . .
>
> Lift up your heart to Him, sometimes even at your meals, and when you are in company; the least little remembrance will always be acceptable to Him. . . . It is not necessary for being with God to be always at church. We may make an oratory of our heart wherein to retire from time to time to converse with Him in meekness, humility and love. . . . Let us begin, then. . . . Have courage. We have but little time to live; you are near sixty-four, and I am almost eighty. Let us live and die with God. [14]

Completely lacking in learning, and wholly deprived of most of earth's coveted privileges, Brother Lawrence's life has nevertheless flowed out in blessing for all subsequent generations. No one knows how many editions there have been of his little book, nor how many millions have read his words. But the ever-widening influence of his life well exemplifies his own statement: "When [God] finds a soul penetrated with a living faith, he pours into it His graces and favors plentifully; there they flow like a torrent which . . . spreads itself with impetuosity and abundance." [15]

In Brother Lawrence the prophecy of Joel, quoted by Peter on the Day of Pentecost, finds striking fulfillment: "Even upon the menservants and the maidservants in those days I will pour out my spirit." [16] And the ancient prophetic word which Christ applied to all his followers, is surely also fulfilled in this his humble disciple: "They shall all be taught by God." [17]

THE SETTING: 17th-century England

THE BOOK: The world-famous allegory of Christian's journey from the City of Destruction to the Celestial Zion

Pilgrim's Progress
John Bunyan

GREATHEART: *But here was great odds, three against one.*

VALIANT-FOR-TRUTH: *'Tis true; but little or more are nothing to him that has the truth on his side.*

Many of the world's great books have been written in prison. The Apostle Paul and the philosopher Boethius, Sir Walter Raleigh and Mahatma Gandhi, Dietrich Bonhoeffer and Martin Luther King, and a host of others have penned undying messages from prison cells. Among these writings, one of the most renowned and beloved is *Pilgrim's Progress* by John Bunyan. The most famous allegory in English literature, it portrays the Christian life as a long and hazardous journey from the City of Destruction to the heavenly Zion. In the course of his narrative Bunyan creates hundreds of characters and scenes which have become everyday words and themes. Few books in all the world have been translated and republished more often. It is a true religious classic, speaking to the heart of everyone on "inward pilgrimage" through this world.

John Bunyan was a Baptist minister in seventeenth-century England, a time still of much religious persecution. He was born at Elstow in central England in 1628, of poor parents, and received very little education. His remarkable mastery of English seems to have come chiefly from the Bible. For a time he worked as a brazier, the same occupation as his father. Then for about two years, in Cromwell's time, he served in the army. During this early period he lived a careless and openly ungodly life. About 1649 he was married to "a woman of piety," and it was especially through two books which she recommended to him that he was led to faith and newness of life in Christ. He became a member of the church in Bedford, and a few years later, in 1659, he began his preaching ministry which, except for his prison years, continued throughout his life, extending at times to many parts of England. Other than these few facts, we know little of his personal life, except that he spent many years in jail for preaching without a license. He died in 1688.

We do know, however, that John Bunyan was a part of the English Baptist tradition always associated with a great love of liberty. Roger Williams, who first established religious freedom in an American colony, and William Carey, the father of modern missions, were a part of this same tradition. And Bunyan in his later ministry showed himself a true defender of religious liberty by advocating the practice of "open church membership"—admitting those who practiced infant baptism as well as those who did not. He authored many books, including his autobiography, *Grace Abounding to the Chief of Sinners,* but only *Pilgrim's Progress,* written during the twelve years he was confined in Bedford jail, has become immortal. It has won fame and acclaim, not only for its literary style and its imaginative genius, but above all for its symbolic portrayal of the varieties of Christian experience. Christians of every denomination, and of every station in life, find their own hearts and experiences reflected again and again along the Pilgrim's way. One contemporary writer describes its universal appeal in these words: "This book has been read in prim parlors, in sophisticated drawing rooms, in royal households, in religion classes, in public schools, in family worship—and still it is read—and will be read forever." [1]

Pilgrim's Progress is written in two parts, "under the similitude of a dream." In Part I the author lies down to sleep in a "den" (representing Bedford jail), and in his dream he catches his first glimpse of the Pilgrim:

> I dreamed, and behold, I saw a man clothed with rags, standing in a certain place, with his face from his own house, a book in his hand, and a great burden upon his back. I looked, and saw him open the book, and read therein; and as he read, he wept and trembled; and, not being able longer to contain, he brake out in a lamentable cry, saying, "What shall I do?" [2]

The Pilgrim's family are of no help to him; rather, they make light of his trouble, and seek to hinder him from leaving his home in the City of Destruction. But his burden is heavy, and he is ready to do anything to be free of it. Walking one day in the fields, reading his book and deeply distressed in spirit, he encounters Evangelist, who advises him to flee, and gives him directions as to where he may find deliverance. He listens and sets forth. Soon he meets others, some of whom try to confuse and mislead him, but he does not permit himself to be distracted. Passing through the Wicket Gate, to which Evangelist has pointed him, and with further guidance from the Interpreter, he comes at length within sight of the cross of Christ. Here is Bunyan's unforgettable picture of a soul finding peace:

> Now, I saw in my dream that the highway up which Christian was to go was fenced on either side with a wall that was called Salvation. Up this way, therefore, did burdened Christian run, but not without great difficulty, because of the load on his back.
>
> He ran thus till he came to a place somewhat ascending; and upon that place stood a cross, and a little below, in the bottom, a sepulchre. So I saw in my dream, that just as Christian came up with the cross, his burden loosed from off his shoulders, and fell from off his back and began to tumble, and so continued

> to do till it came to the mouth of the sepulchre, where
> it fell in, and I saw it no more.
>
> Then was Christian glad and lightsome, and said
> with a merry heart, "He hath given me rest by His sor-
> row, and life by His death." [3]

Following the portrayal of Christian's initial spiritual crisis
and liberation, Bunyan continues to present, in a steady stream
of symbolic pictures, a wide variety of struggles, tribulations,
defeats, and victories which mark the Christian way.

We can only mention a few of the many experiences, good and
bad, that come to him. Shortly after leaving home, he had met
Obstinate and Pliable, representing contrasting false attitudes
toward the claims of religion. Now he soon encounters Apollyon,
the armored fiend from the Pit, who "made at him, throwing
darts as thick as hail." [4] Christian is wounded, but the combat
continues on for a half day. At one point Christian loses his
sword, but then skillfully regains it, and finally gives Appolyon
"a deadly thrust, which made him give back, as one that had
received a mortal wound." [5]

A major source of help and blessing to Christian along his
way is the friendship of two men who become his close companions: first Faithful, and then, after Faithful's tragic death, Hopeful. One day as he and Faithful are walking along together, they
are joined by an apparent "fellow-pilgrim," named Talkative,
who is indeed very orthodox in his conversation, but full of
empty words. When Faithful is beginning to be deceived, Christian enlightens him:

> This man with whom you are so taken will beguile
> with this tongue of his twenty of them that know him
> not. . . . He talketh of prayer, of repentance, of faith,
> and of the new birth; but he knows but only to talk
> of them. . . . His house is as empty of religion as the
> white of an egg is of savor.[6]

As Faithful continues his conversation with Talkative, the falsity
of the latter's religion is clearly revealed. At the end he calls

Faithful a "peevish or melancholy man not fit to be discoursed with," [7] and leaves him.

The pilgrims meet other characters who likewise seek to divert them from the truth. Atheist laughs at them when they say they are going to Mount Zion, a place he says does not even exist. Mr. Money-love gives a clever defense both of the minister who so manipulates things that he can get a better salary, and of the merchant who uses religion to improve his business. Ignorance is proud of his honesty and morality, but counsels the pilgrims to "follow the religion of your own country, and I will follow the religion of mine." [8] Objections and opposition to the Christian way take a thousand different forms.

Arriving at Vanity Fair, a huge marketplace where all the goods and pleasures of the world are on display, the pilgrims do not conform to the ways of the patrons of the Fair—neither in speech, nor in dress, nor in manner. They disparage both the "riches" and the activities going on around them. When they refuse to change, they are arrested and brought to trial before the judge, Lord Hategood. False witnesses accuse them, the jury adjudges them guilty, and Faithful, who has spoken out with special boldness, is condemned "to be put to the most cruel death that could be invented." [9] As he dies, the author sees that "a chariot and a couple of horses carry him up through the clouds with sound of trumpet the nearest way to the Celestial Gate." [10] Christian is sent back to prison, but after a time gains his release.

Not long after these sad events Christian is joined by Hopeful. They have good fellowship, but unfortunately, they very soon yield to the temptation to turn off the highway through Bypath Meadow because the way there seems shorter. This leads to their capture by Giant Despair, who throws them into the dark dungeon of Doubting Castle. He flogs them mercilessly, showing them the bones of earlier pilgrims who have died at his hand, and at last tells them to commit suicide. In their misery they even consider this, but are deterred by the Word of God. After days of suffering, earnest prayer leads them to remember that they do have a key of Promise which will open the doors of the castle. Thus they escape, and are soon back on the King's Highway.

Not all the experiences of the pilgrims, however, involve temptation and suffering. Many people give them help and encouragement. Early in his journey, for instance, Pilgrim visits the House Beautiful, built by the Lord of the Hill for the relief and security of pilgrims. Here he meets the three beautiful sisters, Piety, Prudence, and Charity, who bid him a warm welcome and invite him to be their guests for the evening meal and the night. They engage in long conversations, especially about the experiences that Christian has had along the way. They also speak much of Christ and of what He has done for them:

> PRUDENCE: And what makes you so desirous to go to Mt. Zion? CHRISTIAN: Why there I hope to see him alive that did hang dead upon the cross; and there I hope to be rid of all those things that to this day are an annoyance to me. There, they say, there is no death, and there I shall dwell with such company as I like best. For . . . I love Him because I was by Him eased of my burden.[11]

On the next day the sisters show him many of the treasures of the House Beautiful, and persuading him to stay yet another day, they direct his vision to the Delectable Mountains in Immanuel's Land in the distance. When he sets forth, he has been so strengthened and inspired by their Christian fellowship, that he is able to face without fear the Valley of Humiliation and other perils of the way.

The journey is long. There are rugged mountains and fierce enemies, yet ever there are refreshing variations as well. Bunyan sketches a multitude of scenes, all interesting, all different, all showing keen psychological and spiritual insight. At last, after many years, Christian and Hopeful draw near to the Holy City and, like all pilgrims, must pass through the dread dark river of death. Bunyan depicts this experience vividly:

> They then addressed themselves to the water; and, entering, Christian began to sink, and crying out to

his good friend Hopeful, he said, "I sink in deep
waters; the billows go over my head; all his waves are
going over me. Selah." Then said the other, "Be of
good cheer, my brother; I feel the bottom, and it is
good." Then said Christian, "Ah, my friend, the sorrows of death have compassed me about." And with
that, a great darkness and horror fell upon Christian.[12]

The two pilgrims in the river struggle on, at times almost completely overcome by doubt and terror. But they encourage each
other by recalling some of the rich promises of Scripture, and
are finally victorious. Christian "found ground to stand upon,
and so it followed that the rest of the river was but shallow.
Thus they got over." [13]

Part II of Pilgrim's Progress tells the parallel story of Christiana, Christian's wife, and her four children, who after a time
also repent and set out on the way to the Celestial City. Early
in their journey Christiana enlists a gentle fellow-pilgrim named
Mercy, and they meet other helpful friends along the way too.
Above all they have the companionship of a special guardian
and guide named Great-Heart, the most inspiring character in
the whole book, a symbol of the Holy Spirit.

Throughout Part II there is a strong emphasis on the blessings of Christian *fellowship,* symbolized by a group of pilgrims
journeying together. Often they are refreshed and encouraged by
other groups along the way. For a whole month they share the
delightful hospitality of the House Beautiful. At the inn where
Gaius is the host their conversation about "their Lord, themselves,
and their journey" lasts through the entire night until daybreak.
Even in the town of Vanity, where Faithful had been cruelly
martyred, they are helped by a small but bold group, all of whom
are like themselves on the way to the Celestial City.

This second group of pilgrims visit many of the same places
as did Christian and his companions, and frequently encounter
similar difficulties and joys. At times their conversations grow
somewhat lengthy, but most of the time the narrative moves on

briskly with fresh examples of Bunyan's biblical symbolism. As
an illustration of how strikingly he clothes profound spiritual
truth in allegorical dress, we may quote snatches of the conversation with Great-Heart as the pilgrims pass through the Valley of Humiliation where Christian had his fierce battle with
Appolyon.

This valley is, above all, the place where pilgrims learn the
grace of humility. It is, therefore, despite the dangers lurking
in its shadows, a very precious place, as we also learn from their
conversation. Great-Heart's opening words calm their fears
aroused by the news of Christian's hard fight:

> We need not be afraid of this valley, for here is noth-
> ing to hurt us unless we procure it to ourselves. . . .
> It is the best and most fruitful ground in all these
> parts. . . . Behold how green this valley is, also how
> beautiful with lilies. I have also known many laboring
> men that have got good estates in this Valley of Hu-
> miliation, for 'God resisteth the proud but giveth
> grace to the humble.' [14]

As they go along, conversing, they come upon a young lad
watching sheep. Suddenly they hear that he is singing and from
his lips come the words of one of Bunyan's most lovely hymns:

> He that is down needs fear no fall,
>   He that is low no pride;
> He that is humble, ever shall
>   Have God to be his guide.[15]

Great-Heart comments: "Do you hear him? I will dare to say
that this boy lives a merrier life, and wears more of that herb
called heart's-ease in his bosom than he that is clad in silk and
velvet." [16]

Continuing the allegory he goes on:

> In this valley our Lord formerly had his country
> house. He loved much to be here. He loved also to
> walk these meadows, . . . Besides, here a man shall
> be free from the noise and from the hurrying of this

life. . . . This is a valley that nobody walks in but those that love a pilgrim's life.[17]

Mercy, Christiana's young companion, responds here, indicating the blessings and benefits which she has found in this valley:

> I think that I am as well in this valley as I have been anywhere else in all our journey; the place, methinks, suits with my spirit. Here one may, without much molestation, be thinking what he is, whence he came, what he has done, and to what the King has called him. . . . They that go rightly through this Valley of Baca make it a well; the rain that God sends down from heaven upon them that are here also filleth the pools.[18]

Great-Heart concludes and summarizes the conversations by quoting the promise of the Lord to Isaiah: "To this man will I look, even to him that is poor and of a contrite spirit." [19] No brighter jewel than humility adorns the Christian's crown, and in the symbolism of the Valley of Humiliation Bunyan graphically portrays it in all its loveliness.

Christiana and her companions, reach the end of their journey after overcoming many obstacles and adversaries. One by one, they too are summoned to come to the Palace of the King. Each one responds in words of victorious, though at times trembling, faith. Mr. Valiant-for-Truth answers the summons with a matchless witness.

> "I am going to my Father's . . . My sword I give to him that shall succeed me in my pilgrimage, and my courage and skill to him that can get it. My marks and scars I carry with me, to be a witness for me that I have fought his battles who will now be my rewarder." So he passed over, and all the trumpets sounded for him on the other side.[20]

The final scene describes the crossing-over of Mr. Standfast, a noble pilgrim-figure who has joined them late in their journey. The river at the moment is calm, and "when he was about

half-way in, [he] stood a while and talked to his companions." [21]
He speaks of his great longing to come at last into the presence
of Christ,

> I am going to see that head which was crowned with
> thorns, . . . and shall be with Him in whose company
> I delight myself. I have loved to hear my Lord spoken
> of; and wherever I have seen the print of his shoe in
> the earth, there I have coveted to set my foot, too. [22]

Here is the authentic pilgrim spirit: complete devotion to the
Savior, eagerness to follow wherever his footsteps lead, stead-
fastness through all the struggles of the way, to the end.

Throughout his whole presentation of the Christian's journey
"from cross to crown," Bunyan's aim is not only to instruct and
entertain, but also to challenge. The pilgrim way is long and
rugged, often full of danger. But the resources of God are ever
at hand. To overcome and arrive safe home at last, it is only
necessary that we be willing to make the decisive choice, to set
forth, to continue in the way. Mr. Valiant-for-Truth puts it best,
in the words of Bunyan's now famous poem:

> He who would valiant be
>   'Gainst all disaster,
> Let him in constancy
>   Follow the Master.
> There's no discouragement
>   Shall make him once relent
> His first avowed intent
>   To be a pilgrim. . . .
>
> Since, Lord, thou dost defend
>   Us with thy Spirit,
> We know we at the end
>   Shall life inherit.
> Then fancies flee away!
>   I'll fear not what men say,
> I'll labor night and day
>   To be a pilgrim. [23]

THE SETTING: 18th-century colonial America

THE BOOK: A Quaker tradesman-minister tells of his faith and his witness against slavery and other social evils

The Journal of John Woolman

I have seen in the Light of the Lord that the day is approaching when the man that is most wise in human policy shall be the greatest fool; and the arm that is mighty to support injustice shall be broken in pieces.

John Woolman's is the most eloquent and persuasive voice in three hundred years of Quaker history in America. His *Journal* is famous both as a document of social protest and as a masterpiece of American literature. Among the spiritual classics of the whole world it stands high because of its unique combining of the two-fold call to a devoted inner life with God and to a life of uncompromising justice and brotherhood toward man. But like the other classics, *The Journal of John Woolman* was not the product of a single life. It was nurtured in the fertile soil of vital fellowship in the Society of Friends.

The Friends, or Quakers, had their beginnings in the middle of the 17th century in the preaching of George Fox. Born in Fenny Drayton, in central England, the son of a weaver, Fox as a young man was burdened by an overwhelming sense of guilt. After seeking help from various religious leaders, but finding none, in great anguish of spirit he turned to seek God in his own heart. In his *Journal* he tells how he found peace.

> When all my hopes in them and in all men were gone,
> so that I had nothing outwardly to help me, . . . then
> I heard a voice which said, "There is one, even Christ
> Jesus, that can speak to thy condition"; and when I
> heard it, my heart did leap for joy.[1]

In that moment the gospel of Christ became for George Fox not only a message written in the Bible and preached about in the church, but a living reality within his own heart. Soon he began to preach, proclaiming the liberating power of Christ which he himself had experienced, and opposing and denouncing the lax ways and "merely doctrinal" preaching prevalent in the churches. Followers gathered round him, attracted by his magnetic personality and his devoted life.

But in England before the Toleration Act of 1689, there was little religious freedom, and soon Fox and his Friends met persecution, arrest, and imprisonment. The Friends, however, were persistent. No persecution could dissuade them from obeying the Light of Christ which they had found. In addition, they strongly emphasized the practice of sincere love toward all men, regardless of creed or status. The latter conviction led them to the total renunciation of war, and to opposition to slavery and to every form of social injustice.

The first great Quaker leader in America was William Penn, who in 1682 founded Pennsylvania as a colony based on Quaker principles, providing religious freedom for all who confessed their faith in God. Through the practice of brotherly love and understanding Penn established friendly relations with the Indians, so that Pennsylvania became in truth a "peaceable kingdom." But it was not to endure. Quakerism gradually grew more compromised in its practices, both in its relations with the Indians and in its attitudes toward the curse of slavery and many other social evils. It was in this setting that the quiet voice of John Woolman became a powerfully prophetic witness, calling the Friends back to their true heritage of faith and practice.

Woolman was born in 1720 in Northampton, New Jersey, and grew up in an atmosphere of simple, devout Quaker life.

For a time he worked for a shopkeeper, meanwhile learning the trade of tailoring. After a while he was able to set up his own small business, which as a result of his natural talent for business soon became quite prosperous, enabling him to give much of his time to traveling and preaching as a self-supported Quaker minister. This relatively independent status freed him to champion unpopular causes and protest against slavery, poverty, and other forms of oppression. And Woolman used his freedom well.

John Woolman's *Journal,* published in 1774, two years after his death, records the story of his life of spiritual ministry and social protest. He began to write it in 1756, when he was 36 years old, but it tells also of the experiences of his earliest childhood, of his quest for peace with God, and of his early awakening to the reality of the evils prevailing around him. The narrative quickly moves on to tell of his lifelong struggle against injustice in many forms. The *Journal* is continued to within a few days of his death, which occurred in England in 1772. Through its simple, often quaintly Quaker, language, we are introduced to an unassuming but powerful life that was to make its mark upon the subsequent history of a whole nation. The *Journal* is not a large book, only a little over 200 pages, but it turns the searchlight of truth on many issues and questions which have troubled the consciences of modern man, not only in America but in our whole developing world.

The institution of slavery early came to be the special and constant object of Woolman's attacks. In the long struggle against Negro slavery in the United States, the words and witness of John Woolman are a shining light of hope and promise. And his *Journal* has a strangely contemporary quality today, when the three problems of *war, race,* and *money* deeply trouble the conscience of America. Woolman spoke convincingly on all these issues.

Moreover, he was profoundly concerned about all human suffering and injustice. The miners and the sailor lads, as well as the enslaved Negroes and the ill-treated Indians, awakened his sympathy and evoked his sharp indictment against oppression. The fear of God seems to have set him utterly free from the fear of man. He saw through the thinly veiled shallowness, injustice, and cruelty which most of his fellow citizens (also within the Society of Friends) simply accepted and condoned.

In a sense, the life recorded in John Woolman's *Journal* was one of narrow compass. He did not travel far—except his last voyage to England, where he died. But he did go on many preaching trips, including one longer journey to the South. And everywhere he went, he engaged in a profound personal ministry. Custom and formality were never highly regarded by him either in ordinary life or in the religious sphere. He sought to bring men face to face with God and his uncompromising claims. A few quotations will reveal how bold and clear-visioned was his thinking.

Concerning slavery, Woolman's conscience was first awakened when, in his capacity as a public scrivener, he was asked to draft a bill of sale for a Negro. He did it, with great reluctance, but afterward he came to see "slave-keeping to be a practice inconsistent with the Christian religion," [2] and vowed, "Never again!" His first involvement was his last. Later he writes of the Negroes:

> These are the people by whose labor the other inhabitants are in great measure supported, and many of them in the luxuries of life. These are the people who have made no agreement to serve us. . . . These are the souls for whom Christ died, and for our conduct toward them we must answer before Him who is no respecter of persons.[3]

He understood clearly the divine judgment that slavery would at last bring upon the nation:

> Many slaves on this continent are oppressed, and their cries have reached the ears of the Most High! . . . Should we now . . . neglect to do our duty in firmness and constancy. . . . God may by terrible things in righteousness answer us in this matter.[4]

Though gentle-hearted and kindly, John Woolman when face to face with evil was as stern and uncompromising as truth.

Regarding the injustices done to the Indians, Woolman's words are equally pointed:

> As I rode over the barren hills my meditations were on the alterations in the circumstances of the natives of this land since the coming in of the English. . . . The natives have in some places, for trifling considerations, sold their inheritance so favorably situated, and in other places have been driven back by superior force. . . . By the extension of English settlements . . . the wild beasts on which the natives chiefly depend for subsistence are not so plentiful as they were, and people too often for the sake of gain, induce them to waste their skins and furs in purchasing a liquor which tends to the ruin of them and their families.[5]

But Woolman was disturbed and aroused by more than such flagrant evils. He became keenly aware of the temptations connected with increasing business enterprises, and after a time he decided to give up his mercantile business, and continue only as a tailor, with no apprentices, in order to devote himself more undividedly to a spiritual service. He saw the dangers involved in all kinds of self-indulgence and luxuries. He noticed a common connection between the "too liberal use of spirituous liquors and the custom of wearing too costly apparel" and vigorously opposed both.[6] As an earnest Quaker, he was of course a strong opponent of war and all violence, but he also understood that the causes of war were usually greed and lust for power. Searchingly he asked himself: am I doing anything, in my manner of life, that will ultimately have the effect of leading to war? Whatever he found to have this result, he gave up.

In every area of life he prized and cultivated an unsullied conscience. Within his heart he struggled earnestly to see "truth" regarding every issue, and likewise in his actions never to compromise what he had come to see was right.

Many might say that he was "over-scrupulous." Once, for example, when he contemplated a trip to the West Indies to look into the condition of the Negroes there, he felt he could not accept passage at the lower fare which was made possible by the illicit trade carried on by these vessels. He gave up the use of sugar because it was produced by slave labor. He wore simple clothes because he saw that luxurious dress often led to pride, conflict, and even war. He prayed to the Lord on behalf of Friends "that He would graciously lead some to be patterns of deep self-denial in things relating to trade and handicraft labor; and that others who have plenty of the treasure of this world may be examples of a plain frugal life, and pay wages to such as they may hire more liberally than is customary in some places." [7]

And in a similar vein he wrote to Friends in North Carolina who were subjected to the twin temptations of slave-holding and a too strong desire for profit:

> Take heed that no views of outward gain get too deep
> hold of you, that so your eyes being single to the Lord,
> you may be preserved in the way of safety. Where peo-
> ple let loose their minds after the love of outward
> things and are more engaged in pursuing the profits
> than to be inwardly acquainted with the way of true
> peace, they walk in a vain shadow.[8]

Always, too, although his own conscience was keen and sensitive, Woolman was anxious to have the judgment of fellow-Christians. After his struggle about accepting passage to the West Indies he went back to his home community in Philadelphia to seek further counsel. In quaint Quaker words he says:

> In the fresh spring of pure love I had some labors in
> a private way among Friends on a subject relating to
> truth's testimony. . . . And I was graciously helped
> to discharge my duty in the fear and dread of the
> Almighty.[9]

Sensitive to the guidance of the Spirit, Woolman paid attention also to his dreams as possible channels of God's speaking to him. In a famous passage in the *Journal*, written in England shortly before his death, he recalls how a few years earlier he had been critically ill with pleurisy, so ill that he could not even remember his own name. Then, through his feverish imaginings, there came to him a symbolic vision of the meaning and message of his life. Here is how he describes it:

> Being then desirous to know who I was, I saw a mass of matter of a dull gloomy color, between the south and the east, and was informed that this mass was human beings in as great misery as they could be, and live, and that I was mixed with them, and that henceforth I might not consider myself as a distinct or separate being. In this state I remained several hours. I was then carried in spirit to the mines, where poor oppressed people were digging rich treasures for those called Christians, and heard them blaspheme the name of Christ, at which I was grieved, for his name to me was precious.[10]

In the midst of this shadowed and gloomy vision Woolman also heard a soft melodious voice as of an angel, saying "John Woolman is dead." When he came to himself, and was informed by those around him that he was really John Woolman, he found himself repeating the verse of Scripture, "I am crucified with Christ, nevertheless I live; yet not I, but Christ liveth in me." [11] He then understood that what the angel had been announcing was the death of John Woolman's *will*. He was no longer to live for himself, but as a wholly dedicated servant of God to be "mixed in" with all mankind.

The *Journal* gives repeated evidence, however, that no matter how strong Woolman's concern was for issues of social and public justice, his central emphasis was upon personal and spiritual values. He believed and practiced the scriptural precept, "Keep your heart with all vigilance, for from it flow the springs of life." [12] In a pointed example of wise spiritual counsel he admonishes himself and his fellow-ministers:

> Thou who sometimes travellest in the work of the ministry and art made very welcome by thy friends,

seest many tokens of their satisfaction in having thee
for their guest. It is good for thee to dwell deep, that
thou mayest feel and understand the spirits of people.
It is needful for us to take heed that their kindness
. . . do not hinder us from the Lord's work.[13]

Yet the *Journal* is a book for all Christians, whatever their
calling, whatever their church affiliation. A striking passage
dated in the Quaker manner, "Fourth of fourth month, 1757"
expresses the author's thoroughly ecumenical spirit.

I have been informed that Thomas à Kempis lived
and died in the profession of the Roman Catholic religion; and, in reading his writings, I have believed
him to be a man of a true Christian spirit, as fully so
as many who died martyrs because they could not join
with some superstitions in that Church. All true Christians are of the same spirit, but their gifts are diverse,
Jesus Christ appointing to each one his peculiar office,
agreeably to his infinite wisdom.[14]

John Woolman served God in his own generation. He was a
voice crying in the wilderness of that colonial time. But his words
—on almost every page—are startlingly pertinent today. Men still
fear to walk in the ways of God, the ways of honesty, unselfish-
ness, truth and love; instead, they seek to subject others to their
will, or to outwit and take some advantage of them. Woolman's
simple ways and guileless Christian practice may never become
popular. But they bear their strong, quiet witness. And here and
there are those who cannot resist, but rise up and follow in the
same path of righteousness. They are the salt of the earth.

THE SETTING: 19th-century Denmark

THE BOOK: A profound philosopher, captured by Christ, summons his readers to spiritual reality and Christian cross-bearing

For Self-Examination
Søren Kierkegaard

Even though we are all baptized, every man may well need to become a Christian in another sense.

The writings of Søren Kierkegaard concerning the spiritual life differ sharply from those of other great devotional writers in at least two respects. In the first place, many of his earlier books deal only *indirectly* with the problems of religious faith; and secondly, all his writing has a strong element of *irony*, aimed at exposing the subtle sins and self-deceptions of the human heart. Living in a nominally Christian land, Kierkegaard came to see the Christianity around him as shallow and hypocritical, a poor imitation of real Christianity. He was brought up in the church and in the "Christian" philosophy of his time, but more and more he turned against them in disillusionment, denounced them, fought against them with tongue and pen. In this struggle he finally gave his life. Broken in body and spirit, he collapsed on the street in his native city, and a few days later died, at the age of only 42.

Hundreds of passages in his devotional books bear witness that few writers can speak more gently to the burdened heart than Søren Kierkegaard. But he saw with uncompromising clarity that if there is to be inward healing there must first be honest heart-searching and penitence. The title of his book, *For Self-Examination*, is significant: before we can come to God we must, like the prodigal, "come to ourselves."

Kierkegaard's tragic life was the soil and setting which nurtured all his writing. Even more than for most authors, therefore, some knowledge of his life can help us to understand his message. He was born in Copenhagen on May 5, 1813, the youngest of seven children. His parents had moved to the city from Jutland some years earlier, and his father had become remarkably successful as a wool merchant, so much so that he was able to retire at the age of 40. He was 55 when Søren was born, and there grew up between them a strong and enduring relationship. But Michael Pedersen Kierkegaard's spirit was one of deep melancholy, and year by year this was imparted to his son. Despite his business success and his fine community standing, the father could not escape the burden of some deeply hidden secrets in his past. Long afterward, Søren learned that one day during his years of poverty as a boy on the Jutland heath, his father had climbed up on a little hill, clenched his fist, looked up to heaven, and cursed God. Ever after, he felt that a curse rested upon him and his family.

So Søren Kierkegaard's life was clouded from the very beginning. Like his father he became a prisoner of melancholy. His whole life experience—the books that he wrote, the struggles that he endured, even his interpretation of the Christian life—all were related to and marked by a sense of the somberness, the suffering, the sorrow of life.

He began his studies at the University of Copenhagen at the age of 17, concentrating on literature, philosophy, and theology. His university years were at a time of intellectual and spiritual struggle. The prevailing philosophical defenses of religion failed to answer his probing questions, and for a time he completely rejected the Christian faith. His moral convictions gave way as well, and he lived a life of self-indulgence and dissipation. Breaking with his father, he moved away from home to a rented apartment. He squandered money on food and drink and clothes and friends, leaving his father to pay the bills. He travelled, step by step, mile by mile, to the far country. Later he called it "the road to perdition."

But the husks of sin and unbelief could not satisfy his soul, and the rationalistic philosophy prevailing at the university left his mind unconvinced. Then, at the age of 25, partly influenced by the writings of the German philosopher Hamann, and stirred by the death of a close friend, he began to turn homeward again toward his childhood faith. The outward expression of this is indicated in the record of a Copenhagen pastor that on "July 6, 1838, S. Kierkegaard came to confession and took communion." [1]

Kierkegaard does not call this experience his "conversion"; to the end of his life he insisted that he was only "becoming" a Christian. But in an entry in his journal, dated May 19, 1838, 10:30 A.M., he speaks of the great joy which had come to him:

> There is such a thing as an indescribable joy which glows through us. . . . Not a joy over this or that, but full jubilation "with hearts and souls and voices": a joy which cools and refreshes like a breeze, a gust of the tradewind which blows from the Grove of Mamre to the eternal mansions. [2]

For a time after this, Kierkegaard considered seeking ordination to the ministry, but this was not to be. He continued his studies, completing his master's degree.

Meanwhile, another overwhelming influence had come into his life. He met and fell in love with a young girl, Regina Olsen. Since she was only 14 years old at the time, he disciplined his affection for several years before beginning to court her. But already during that time the thought of her brought him inspiration, profound reason for living and working. They became engaged early in 1841.

But almost immediately thereafter, Kierkegaard began to feel that the engagement had been a mistake. He saw himself as completely unfit for marriage (what all his reasons were have been the subject of study and debate for more than a hundred years), and despite Regina's deep love and the urgent counsel of her parents, he set about to create a situation that would lead her to break the engagement. His plan was successful; the engagement was broken off in 1843. But this strange episode in Kierkegaard's life became far more than an episode. It became the single most far-reaching influence in the rest of his life.

The broken engagement initiated twelve years of continuous writing and publication. Books, large and small, poured from his pen. At first they were books chiefly of philosophy, which sought to analyze the meaning of human life at all its levels, books which for a century have gained an ever-widening readership, books whose purpose was to show indirectly, deviously, but convincingly, that *the essence of life is to live, not to think or talk about living.*

After passing through another major spiritual crisis in 1848, which gave him renewed assurance of "being drawn near to God," Kierkegaard entered upon the second—and final—phase of his authorship. Now the themes in his writing became exclusively devotional, addressed not primarily to the mind but to the heart and will.

Among these devotional books one of the most heart-searching is *For Self-Examination,* published in 1851, only four years before his death. Though written in simple language, it is a powerful example of Kierkegaard's life-long insistence that the chief thing in the Christian religion is *life, not words; practice, not mere profession.* A story from one of his earlier books vividly illustrates this point:

> It is said to have chanced in England that a traveller was attacked on the highway by a robber who had made himself unrecognizable by wearing a big wig. He falls upon the traveller, seizes him by the throat and shouts, "Your purse!" He gets the purse and keeps it, but the wig he throws away. A poor man comes along the same road, puts it on and arrives at the next town where the traveller has already denounced the

crime, he is arrested, is (mistakenly) recognized by the traveller, who takes his oath that he is the man. By chance the robber is present in the courtroom, sees the misunderstanding, turns to the judge and says, "It seems to me that the traveller has regard rather to the wig than to the man." [3]

So it is in Christendom, says Kierkegaard. Men pay attention to the wig instead of to the man—to outward profession, not to inward reality.

For Self-Examination consists of three sermons, on the texts for the 5th Sunday after Easter, Ascension Day, and Pentecost. In the first we are brought face to face with God the Father, in the second with the Son, in the third with the Holy Spirit.

The text of the first sermon is from the Epistle of James:

> If any one is a hearer of the word, and not a doer, he is like a man who observes his natural face in a mirror; for he observes himself, and goes away and at once forgets what he was like. [4]

James is sometimes said to teach a "gospel of works." But Kierkegaard immediately launches into a denunciation, not of works, but of a false reliance upon God's grace:

> There is always a worldliness that is desirous of having the name of being a Christian but wishes to become one at as cheap a price as possible. [5]

> True faith, however, "is a turbulent thing. It is health, but it is stronger and more violent than the most burning fever." [6]

But how are we to become such real Christians—with a "turbulent" inner faith that also expresses itself in a true outward life of witness? The basic answer, says Kierkegaard, lies in a right use of the Word of God.

> The first requirement is that you must not look at the
> mirror and inspect the mirror, but see yourself in the
> mirror.[7]

So much time and effort and learning have been expended in
study *about* the Bible: Who were the authors? are they reliable?
have they themselves seen what they write about? And then the
30,000 different interpretations! If I permit myself to be taken up
with all these questions—studying the mirror—I may never get
around to seeing *myself* in the mirror.

Actually, says Kierkegaard, the Bible is to be treated like a
love letter from a loved one. In the reading of any love letter
heart speaks to heart. So must it be with one's reading of the
Bible. Even the learned professors must read it in this way—not
simply study the mirror. "Be sure to remember that when you
read God's Word learnedly, with a dictionary, etc., you are not
reading God's Word." [8] "If you are not learned, do not envy the
scholar. Rejoice that you can begin reading God's Word at
once!" [9] And if there are obscure passages in the Bible, do not
be concerned about that. "It is not the obscure passages that
bind you, but those which you understand." [10]

Kierkegaard has only scathing rebuke for mere "interpretation" of the Bible:

> All this interpretation and interpretation and science
> and new science is produced on the solemn, grave
> principle that it is for rightly understanding God's
> Word. Look more closely and you will see that it is
> to defend itself against God's Word—in about the
> same way as a boy who puts one or more napkins in
> his trousers when he is to get a thrashing.[11]

A further fundamental requirement for seeing oneself in the
mirror is to constantly say to oneself: *"It is talking to me; I am
the one it is speaking about."* [12] As Nathan pressed home to
David the accusing word, "Thou art the man," so must we let
the Word press its message home to our hearts: *I* am the one
who is concerned here. Our hearts are deceptive. We do not

want to face the truth. We do not dare to look in the mirror. It is more pleasant to study it. But if we dare to look in the mirror in our reading, then

> sometimes you will read a fear and trembling into your soul, and, by God's help, you will succeed in becoming a man, a personality. You will be saved from being this horrible nonentity into which we human beings—created in God's image—have been bewitched, an impersonal objective something.[13]

And finally, having read, we must not forget what we looked like, but must go immediately, and obey. Here, too, we are deceptive. We are tempted to be like the drunkard who thinks he will stop drinking tomorrow. But we must deal sternly with our deceptive hearts and obey *now!*

The text for the second sermon, on Ascension Day, is from the first chapter of Acts, and the theme is "Christ is the way." Once more Kierkegaard strikes the keynote: in Christianity, words must be rooted in life. Christ is the way because his life exemplified what he taught. The way is narrow. Christ's life *was* "narrow" from the very beginning: he did not just *say* the way is narrow. He was born in poverty. Already as a child he was persecuted by the rulers. As he grew older, the way was still narrow and difficult. He had no place to lay his head. And always he was surrounded by temptation, not only in the desert, but all the way. The greatest temptation of all was to compromise, to say less about himself than was true, to lower the standards for his followers. And ever before him lay the shadow of the cross. He loved his people, and served them; but he knew that his very work of love was playing a part in bringing him to the cross.

The way became narrower and narrower as it progressed—all the way to death. Little by little it became clear that he must "cast fire upon the earth": [14] his life and teachings would divide people, brother from brother, father from son—in all generations. This was the bitterest cup of all. Yet he had to drink it, for love's sake. Death inescapable. Judas. Gethsemane. Calvary. Forsaken by God and man. The way was narrow, ever, ever narrower—to the end.

Then came the Ascension—but only then. It was glorious, eternally glorious, but only *after death*. And that death was self-chosen.

Christ was not one who aspired to wealth, but had to be satisfied with poverty. He *chose* poverty. And all who would follow him must *choose* the narrow way. They must imitate Christ. They must be identified with him. How complete this identification is between Christ and the believer comes to clear expression in Kierkegaard's description of what it means to pray in the name of Jesus:

> I cannot pray in the name of Jesus to have my own will; . . . the fact that the name of Jesus Christ comes at the beginning is not prayer in the name of Jesus; but it means to pray in such a manner that I dare name Jesus in it; that is to say, think of him, think of his holy will together with what I am praying for; . . . it means . . . Jesus assumes the responsibility and all the consequences, he steps forward for us, steps into the place of the person praying.[15]

Sometimes we may be tempted to doubt the reality of the Ascension, to doubt that Christ is really the victor who has overcome death. So it was for the apostles. What they suffered in following Christ purged them of every doubt. *The proof of Christianity is not in argument but in the experience of following Christ.* We are like the ten lepers: "as they went, they were cleansed." [16]

> And you, my listener, what do you do? Do you doubt the Ascension? If so, then do as I do. Say to yourself, "Well, this doubt is nothing to fuss about. I know very well where and how it came—from this, that I must have been careful of myself in regard to *imitating*, that my life is not exerted enough in this direc-

tion, that I have too easy a life, that I spare myself the risks which are bound up with witnessing for the truth and against untruth." [17]

Kierkegaard's final assertion concerning the Ascension is simple and strong: when one suffers because one does good, because one is right, because one is loving—when it is for a good cause that one lives forsaken, persecuted, mocked, impoverished—then one will not doubt his Ascension, for one will need it! [18]

In the third sermon, for Pentecost Day, the day of the Holy Spirit, Kierkegaard begins ironically by saying that of course we believe in "the spirit of the age," "the world-spirit," "the human spirit"—all these are commonly accepted and are often casually referred to in conversation.[19] But when we are asked to speak of the Holy Spirit, we hesitate. And perhaps it is right we should, for "one cannot talk about there being a Holy Spirit and believing in a Holy Spirit without binding oneself by one's words." [20] To speak of the Holy Spirit seems to put us in touch with a world which lays solemn claim upon us. Pentecost is a day of deep and powerful earnestness.

Christianity, it is true, issues a universal invitation to life. And man eagerly clings to the life instinct. "Bring us life!" we cry. But Kierkegaard, the watchman on the walls of spiritual reality, sternly interposes:

> This life-giving in the Spirit is not a direct heightening of the natural life in a man, a spontaneous continuation in direct connection with the natural life— blasphemy! How dreadful to take Christianity in vain this way. . . . No, it is a new life, literally a new life— for mark this well, death goes between. . . . You must die, and the life-giving Spirit is the very one which kills you![21]

The Apostles and the first Church had to turn their backs on all the world; they had to die to every human confidence and human

hope. After the cross—Christ's cross and their cross—came Pentecost. And so it must be with us.

And this dying must be a matter of free personal choice, personal renunciation. At this point Kierkegaard draws upon his
own bitter experience of renouncing his betrothed, and describes
the lover's agony in freely choosing to give up his beloved:

> To be obliged to deprive oneself of the one he yearns
> for and now possesses—that is to wound selfishness at
> the root, as in the case of Abraham when God de-
> manded that Abraham himself—how dreadful—with
> his own hand—horror and madness!—offer Isaac.[22]

To freely give up, renounce, wholly surrender—this is what God
requires. Then Pentecost can come. Christianity inevitably involves the suffering of being delivered from selfishness. There is
no escape, no alternative. To live we must die.

But then comes the life-giving Spirit. And then he can pour
out upon us his rich gifts: faith and hope and love—not the faith
and hope and love which are the natural attributes of human
life, but the faith and hope and love flowing from the new life
in the Spirit. Only these can in truth overcome and win the
victory over the world. When the apostles had "died," when
they had had

> the dreadful experience that love is not loved, that it
> is hated, ridiculed, spit on, crucified in this world,
> and crucified while justice in the judgment seat calm-
> ly washes its hands and while the people's voice clam-
> ors for the robber, . . . by loving God they united
> themselves, so to speak, with God to love this world.[23]

Such is the mystery, the transforming mystery of Christian love—
the mystery of the Spirit, the victorious mystery of Pentecost.

With a beautiful story Kierkegaard illustrates once more the
truth which he never tires of reiterating: that the Christian life
must be one of earnest discipline—but to live under the discipline of the Holy Spirit is to know life at its highest and best.

Once upon a time there was a rich man who brought from abroad, at an exorbitant price, a team of faultless and excellent horses which he wanted for his own pleasure and the pleasure of driving them himself.

A year or two passed by. If anyone who had known these horses in earlier days now saw them driven by their owner, he would not be able to recognize them. Their eyes had become dull and drowsy; their pace had no carriage and consistency. They could bear nothing; they could endure nothing. . . . Moreover, they had acquired all sorts of quirks and bad habits. Although they of course got food in abundance, they grew thinner day by day.

The rich man called in the king's coachman. He drove them for one month. At the end of the period there was no team of horses in the whole land which carried their heads so proudly, whose eyes were so fiery, whose pace was so beautiful. . . . How did this happen? The owner, who was no coachman and merely played the coachman, drove the horses according to the horses' conception of how they should be driven. The royal coachman drove them according to a coachman's conception of driving.[24]

Having given this stern challenge to all who would live the Spirit-filled and Spirit-controlled life, Kierkegaard closes the book with this gentle and moving prayer:

O Holy Spirit, we pray for ourselves and for all men— Holy Spirit, Thou who givest life. Here there is no want of capabilities, of culture, of wisdom—rather there is too much of it. But what is wanted is that Thou shouldst take away that which exists for our ruin, take power from us in order to give us life. No doubt, when Thou dost take power from a man in order to become a power in him, it does not happen without a shudder, like the shudder of death. But if even animal creatures later came to understand how good it was for them that the royal coachman took the reins, though at first they surely were struck with terror and their minds rebelled in vain, should a human being then not quickly come to understand what a blessing it is for man that Thou dost take away the power and give life! [25]

THE SETTING: 19th-century Orthodox Russia

THE BOOK: The experience of a "wanderer for Christ" who found the secret of prayer without ceasing

The Way of a Pilgrim
Anonymous

The calling upon the name of Jesus gladdened my way. . . . And that is how I go about now, and ceaselessly repeat the Prayer of Jesus, which is more precious to me than anything in the world.

In the year 1054 occurred a tragic break between the Christian churches of the East and West. Thereafter for more than 900 years there was no official fraternal contact between these two great divisions of Christendom, the Orthodox East and the Roman Catholic West, each regarding itself as the true heir and representative of Apostolic Christianity. The two churches went their separate ways, each developing a distinctive theology, liturgy, architecture, and piety. In the 16th century the Western Church experienced a second great separation in the Protestant Reformation, and Christendom was fractured into three large divisions. Both Catholics and Protestants remained largely unfamiliar with the historical patterns, the writings, and the spirituality of Eastern Orthodoxy. Only within our own generation has this gulf begun to be bridged, and we are slowly learning to know one another.

In an attempt to account for the differences in piety, it is sometimes said that Roman Catholicism takes St. Peter as its leader and stresses authority, Protestantism follows St. Paul and stresses individual experience, while Eastern Orthodoxy, following the spirit of St. John, stresses *sobornost,* or love and community in Christ. Such a classification is oversimplified, but at least it rightly points toward the "spirit" that is characteristic of the church in the East—an emphasis on love and humility and fellowship in Christ. In a number of Orthodox countries there existed for centuries a close alliance between state and church, sometimes actually involving the church in real bondage. But even then, beneath and beyond the outward structure and organizations, a warm life of spiritual love and fellowship often flourished in hundreds of monasteries, in the local congregations, and in the homes of the faithful.

One distinctive mark of Orthodox piety, especially in Russia, is *kenoticism,* referring to a *self-emptying,* taking the lowest place, following the example of Christ, who "emptied himself" and took the form of a servant. For centuries Russian Christians have honored the ideal of poverty and humility as the highest form of Christ-like life. All the great saints of Russia have been marked by this quality. Typical were Boris and Gleb, the royal brothers who permitted themselves to be killed rather than fight for the throne against their brother, and who became the first canonized Russian saints. But there were hundreds of others who lived lives of great holiness and humility, some of whose stories have never been written or told. For us in the West, this remains an almost totally unexplored world of spiritual treasures.

Much of Orthodox spirituality has been centered in the monasteries. In the East there were no religious orders, such as there are in the Roman Catholic Church; each community was self-governing, under the leadership of an abbot. In the monasteries, too, there were often *startsi,* elders of great spiritual insight, to whom people of all classes came for counsel. The figure of Father Zossima in Dostoyevsky's *The Brothers Karamazov* is an unforgettable example of a saintly Russian *starets.*

In old Russia another common religious pattern was "going on pilgrimage." There were thousands of pilgrims who left home

and family and set forth to seek a deeper life with God. Some
had a definite destination, such as Jerusalem or Kiev, but often
the "wandering life" was adopted simply as a means of breaking
off old contacts and reducing daily needs to a level where they
could be met by incidental labor or by the charity of others.
Among the pilgrims and in the monasteries there was a widespread use of the Jesus Prayer, a simple and beautiful form of
devotion developed earlier among Greek-speaking monks in the
Near East.

The Way of a Pilgrim gives us a delightful introduction to
this spirituality as it was found in 19th-century Russia. This
book by an anonymous writer was first published in Kazan in
1884. It purports to be a journal of a penniless pilgrim who
travels among the Russian and Siberian villages and through
the countryside, receiving food and lodging as it is given to him,
conversing with many different types of people, always seeking
the secret of a deeper, more continuous life of prayer. The opening paragraph sets the scene:

> By the grace of God I am a Christian man, by my ac-
> tions a great sinner, and by calling a homeless wan-
> derer of the humblest birth who roams from place to
> place. My worldly goods are a knapsack with some
> dried bread in it on my back, and in my breastpocket
> a Bible. And that is all.[1]

The title, *The Way of a Pilgrim,* has a two-fold meaning: on
the one hand, it tells about the way the Pilgrim travelled and
whom he met, but it also describes the particular way of prayer
which he learned and practiced. The book captures the reader's
attention at once—by its utter simplicity, by its depth of spiritual
insight, and not least by the stream of varied and interesting
personalities the Pilgrim encounters.

The Pilgrim's early life was one of unhappiness. He was or-
phaned in childhood. When he was seven, one arm was crippled
through the carelessness of his only brother. This brother later,
when they are grown, steals the Pilgrim's inheritance and burns

down his house. The Pilgrim marries, but life is grim with hardship, and after but a few years his wife dies. In sorrow and loneliness he then gives away his few possessions, and sets out on a wandering life, at first with no particular goal or motive.

One day in church he hears a sermon on the text, "Pray without ceasing." [2] The words puzzle him. How can it be possible to pray at all times? Burdened by the question, he sets out to find a solution. His first inquiries bring wholly unsatisfactory answers, but at last he encounters a gentle *starets* who undertakes to teach him to pray the Jesus Prayer, that is, to repeat over and over again, either audibly or silently, "Lord Jesus Christ, Son of God, have mercy on me, a sinner." By concentration and long practice, the Pilgrim finds that this prayer becomes almost second nature to him. He can say it thousands of times a day without difficulty. After a period of time, he finds himself praying it even in his sleep.

To those of us who have had no experience of this prayer, it may at first seem mechanical and lacking in meaning. But such was not the experience of the Pilgrim; rather, it brought him great joy. Here is how he describes the effect of the prayer upon him:

> Sometimes my heart would feel as though it were bubbling with joy; such lightness, freedom, and consolation were in it. Sometimes I felt a burning love for Jesus Christ and for all God's creatures. . . . Sometimes that sense of a warm gladness in my heart spread throughout my whole being and I was deeply moved as the fact of the presence of God everywhere was brought home to me.[3]

He repeatedly assures us, too, that the Jesus Prayer is by no means only for monks or religious, but also for every lay person, like himself, who is willing to learn.

Once he has learned this secret of joyous intensive prayer, the Pilgrim gladly shares it with any one along his way who will listen to him. As he travels from village to village, the people whom he meets are many and varied—rich and poor, old and young, good citizens and lawbreakers. The Pilgrim himself is a constant learner from life; often, too, he becomes a teacher, especially by exemplifying a constant spirit of humble gratitude to both men and God. He writes:

> During my wanderings . . . I happened to pass through a certain country town. My supply of dried bread had run very low, so I went to one of the houses to ask for some more. The householder said, "Thank God, you have come just at the right moment, my wife has only just taken the bread out of the oven, so there is a hot loaf for you. Remember me in your prayers." I thanked him and was putting the bread away in my knapsack, when his wife, who was looking on, said, "What a wretched state your knapsack is in, it is all worn out. I'll give you another instead." And she gave me a good strong one. . . . I rejoiced in spirit and thanked God for leading me, unworthy as I was, to such kindly folk. "Now," thought I, "without having to worry about food I shall be filled and content for a whole week. Bless the Lord, O my soul!" [4]

Often the Pilgrim reports a conversation that is rich in both sound thinking and spiritual insight. In one such instance, he has been visiting with a young priest who has invited him to dinner. In response to a question the priest sets forth this instructive method of meditation and prayer:

> To become a man of recollected interior life, you should take some one text or other of Holy Scripture and for as long a period as possible concentrate on that alone all your power of attention and meditation; then the light of understanding will be revealed to you. You must proceed the same way about prayer. If you want it to be pure, right, and enjoyable, you must choose some short prayer consisting of few but forcible words, and repeat it frequently and for a long time. Then you will find delight in prayer. [5]

We in the West are perhaps a bit prejudiced against such repe-
tition in our prayers, but anyone who tries out these directions
will find that they are indeed helpful and have the wisdom of
long experience.

But actually, the totality of prayer is much more inclusive than
these simple practices. In one of the Pilgrim's conversations, in
a home where he is a guest, he reads to his host this quotation
from one of the Fathers, Peter of Damascus:

> The Apostle says, *"Pray without ceasing."* That is,
> he teaches men to have the remembrance of *God* in all
> times and places and circumstances. If you are making
> something, you must call to mind the Creator of all
> things; if you see the light, remember the Giver of it.
> . . . If you put on your clothes, recall Whose gift they
> are and thank Him Who provides for your life. In
> short, let every action be a cause of your remember-
> ing and praising God, and lo! you will be praying
> without ceasing and therein your soul will always
> rejoice.[6]

On another occasion when a fellow pilgrim expresses a strong
aversion for the Jews, the *starets* with whom they are visiting
rebukes him with a wisdom that gives a genuine Christian
answer to anti-Semitism:

> You have no right, friend, to abuse and curse the
> Jews like this. God made them just as he made us. The
> disgust that you feel for them comes from the fact
> that you are not grounded in the love of God and
> have no interior prayer as a security, and therefore,
> no inward peace. The soul which is inwardly united
> to God becomes, in the greatness of its joy, like a
> good-natured, simple-hearted child, and now con-
> demns no one, Greek, heathen, Jew, nor sinner.[7]

In an especially moving incident, the Pilgrim is able to convince a deserter from the army who has also become a thief and
drunkard, to try the simple way of prayer, and thereby to find

his way back to God and a renewed joy in life. The transforming power of the Gospel is constantly in action through him.

Though the Pilgrim has no automatic solution for the ills of
human life, his direct and guileless application of the gospel to
dozens of difficult situations gives an inspiring portrayal of the
working of Russian piety. It is no doubt true, as the Orthodox
scholar, Professor G. P. Fedotov, has pointed out that, "The
author has not the intention of depicting life around him as it
is, but that of selecting instructive examples of Christian virtue." [8] In other words, the piety described was by no means
universal in old Russia. Nevertheless, the picture given is a true
one.

In the last two sections of the book the form of presentation
changes from narrative to dialog. The Pilgrim has encountered
an interesting and earnest fellow-traveller, a professor, and together they go to visit a *starets* again, to seek his counsel. The
latter has other visitors too, and the group is led into an extended
discussion of various aspects of the prayer life. Each of the speak-
ers has his own characteristic approach: the professor, keen and
searching in his questions; the *skhimnik* (a monk of advanced
spiritual experience), profound and wise in counsel; the hermit,
understanding and explaining the values of the solitary life;
the *starets,* a gentle man of deep faith who presides graciously
over the whole discussion. Altogether, they form a group of men
pursuing a topic of great importance, the whole discussion having an involved, Russian flavor. The learning revealed in some of
the speeches indicates that this part of *The Way of a Pilgrim*
cannot be the work of an uneducated peasant, though perhaps
the background document on which it is based may have been
such a pilgrim journal.

The discussants take up again the question of what prayer
actually is, and the answer given is clear and helpful—and
characteristically Russian:

> Truly to pray is to direct the thought and the memory
> without relaxing, to the recollection of God, to walk

in His divine Presence, to awaken oneself to His love
by thinking about Him, and to link the name of God
with one's breathing and the beating of one's heart.
[The earnest seeker after God] is guided in all this by
the invocation of the lips of the most Holy name of
Jesus Christ, or by saying the Jesus Prayer at all times
and in all places and during every occupation, un-
ceasingly.[9]

An especially difficult question, regarding the necessity and
value of intercessory prayer, is pointedly raised by the professor
and helpfully illuminated by the *skhimnik*. The explanation
given is based upon the influence that one personality can have
upon another. In prayer we bring to bear the finest, highest
influences upon those for whom we pray. Clearly and convincingly, the skhimnik shows that we are by no means to *convince* God,
but rather to *work with* him. Contemporary psychologists could
learn much from the wisdom of the *skhimnik*.

An equally perplexing question, especially for modern Western Christians, also raised by the professor, regarding the value
of silence and solitude in the life of prayer, is most helpfully
discussed by the hermit. Human service, he says, is not rendered
only through direct personal contact; sometimes the greatest
help is conveyed through the hidden service of love and intercession. The world is bound together, not only physically, but
spiritually. The hermit, the soul in solitude, adds to the spiritual
riches of the whole world and renews the very springs of life.
At the end, the hermit quotes an anonymous spiritual writer
who even contends that

> if the State were developed to the highest degree of
> education and morals, yet even then it would still be
> necessary to provide people for contemplation, in ad-
> dition to the general activities of the citizen, in order
> to preserve the spirit of truth . . . to keep it for the
> generations to come and hand it on to posterity.[10]

The dialog comes to an end as the Pilgrim and the professor
leave to set out again on their journey to a monastery in the far

North, asking that the others pray for them on their way. Finally, the *starets* pronounces a beautiful scriptural benediction.

Not many of us today would be drawn to adopt the outward life-style of the Pilgrim, nor perhaps even to follow the forms of prayer and meditation recommended in his book. Contemporary America is far removed from 19th-century Russia. But the *inner essence* of the Pilgrim's life pattern is certainly worthy of our study and our pursuit: an earnest desire for spiritual instruction, a continuing hidden life of prayer, simplicity of life and honesty of speech, brotherliness and helpfulness toward all whom we meet, sincere participation in the life of the church, faith in divine guidance along life's way. These are priceless spiritual qualities which we all do well to seek and to cultivate. For all who desire to have a part in this high quest, the Pilgrim's ways and words can be a perennially inspiring guide.

THE SETTING:	20th-century Australia and England
THE BOOK:	Essays on the principles and practice of prayer

Creative Prayer
E. Herman

There comes a moment when we realize that our work for God is a shoddy, futile business, unless it is backed at every point by the apostolate of prayer.

Spiritual classics have their origin in many and diverse places—in the scholar's study, in the quiet of a monastery, along pilgrim ways, in prison cells. *Creative Prayer,* by E. Herman, is the product of a modern Presbyterian manse and a journalist's office. Though not yet as well known as some of the older spiritual classics, it is freighted with the same themes concerning the deeper life with God, analyzed and clarified by a singularly keen and dedicated mind. Together with her minister-husband Mrs. Herman served first in Constantinople, then in Australia, where she gained recognition as a journalist through a column she edited in *The Australian Christian World.* When the Hermans returned to London, she served on the staffs of several outstanding religious journals, her writing soon becoming widely known for both its striking style and its penetrating spiritual insight.

Besides her journalistic work and her spiritual writing Mrs. Herman published two books in the philosophical-religious field.

Thus both her life and her writing were constantly nourished and formed by serious intellectual discipline. She read widely in English, French, German, and Latin. One who knew her intimately wrote, in a tribute published after her death, "Hers was a mind of supreme and piercing ability, of keenest analytic and critical quality." [1]

Yet her life was by no means narrowly intellectual in its interests. She participated actively in the life of her church; she loved social life and conversation, where she could also exercise her rare gifts of humor and sparkling wit; she was an avid and gifted letter writer; among her recreations she lists "country rambles" and "folklore." But her interests and her activities alike were centered in the spiritual—and the spiritual was centered in Christ. In her later years she became a member of the Anglican church (taking Brigid as a new Christian name), but this was only a further step in the development of her essentially ecumenical outlook, so well expressed in one of her essays:

> The Way which is in Christ is no private way. It is the King's Highway. . . . On it we meet the sweeping winds of divine purpose, and the details of doctrinal conviction and practical methods drop into their proper subordinate places.[2]

Throughout her books her teaching is not sectarian, but totally Christian. And as her teaching was, so also was her life and character. Concerning the Anglo-Catholic period in her life, Dr. Duncan Macgregor writes:

> The beautiful humility always characteristic of her was deeper than ever before. The unselfishness of her dealings, and her spirit of self-sacrifice also, became more notable. She practiced asceticism, cared nothing for comfort, and was not too careful even about health. She was filled with a great and burning passion for the Person of Christ, and gave herself with a full abandonment to the service of Christ and her fellows.[3]

Mrs. Herman died on December 2, 1923 at the age of only 48.

Creative Prayer, published in 1921, gives us the mature fruit of her thought. After but a half-century it has won for itself a place among the classics of the spiritual life. Rather than engage in lengthy comments or attempt any full summary of its thought and teaching, we shall call attention to some of its major emphases, and in a number of key passages let the author speak to us directly on the great themes with which she deals.

She begins with a discussion of what prayer really is. Prayer is not a half-magic way of achieving our own goals. Nor is it a method of putting ourselves "into tune with the energies of the universe," as some modern writers have taught. It is not a form of begging or pleading; rather, "Prayer in its essence is communion with God. The simplest analogy—that of loving, trustful intercourse between friend and friend—is also the most profound." [4] All of the beneficent results of the prayer life flow from this central reality. Mrs. Herman illustrates the transforming effect of prayer by a striking comparison with the effect of a true human friendship:

> As we are initiated into the mystery of friendship, we know that our friend is not merely "another"; he speaks to us not from without but from the center of our being. He is in us and we in him. . . . No merely temperamental affinity can account for friendship at its highest potency. Deep down in the abysmal mystery of being was the thread spun that linked soul to soul. My friend creates me and recreates me. His love and trust purge me of sin by shame and contrition, his gentleness makes me great, his high expectations make all things possible to me. And what is true in a limited measure of human friendship is wholly true of man's communion with his Creator. [5]

Among the essential aspects of a true prayer life Mrs. Herman stresses 1) the cultivation of silence, 2) full surrender to God, 3) spiritual discipline, and 4) inward transformation. Concerning the first of these she says:

> The saints were capable of spiritual silence simply

because they had not contracted our modern habit of ceaseless talk in their ordinary life. Their days were days of silence, relieved by periods of conversation, while ours are a wilderness of talk with a rare oasis of silence.

It is useless to imagine that one can pass at a bound from a daily round in which the lust of talk absorbs three-fourths of the soul's energy to a state of harmonious revealing stillness. The practice of silence must begin, not in the "quiet hour" or in the fellowship-meeting, but in the office and the home, the playing field and the Church.[6]

From a cultivation of true silence can come a tremendous sense of peace and power:

Everyone who knows anything about the interior life knows that there is indeed a moment in our communion with God in which the soul knows itself to be alone with Him in the world, and knows also that in that august aloneness lie peace and power. It was in His hours of solitary communion with the Father that Jesus heard the cry of the world's life and looked deep into its heart.[7]

Such can also be our experience. Deep personal prayer is not an escape from the world, but rather a profound entering into the needs and sorrows (as well as the joys!) of other people.

The solitary worshipper who really touches God, and touches him not with a merely self-regarding motive, but with a heart of love for all men and a tender fellow-feeling with human need and woe, is engaged in a more genuine act of fellowship than a thousand gregarious individuals who mistake external togetherness for vital unity.[8]

Concerning the full surrender to God, which is both the result of and the further preparation for prayer, Mrs. Herman quotes a great French spiritual writer, J. N. Grou:

> To give heart and mind to God so that they are ours
> no longer; to do good without being conscious of it;
> to pray ceaselessly and without effort, as we breathe;
> to love without stopping to reflect upon our feelings;
> to go ever onward without pausing to measure our
> progress—such is the perfect forgetfulness of self which
> casts us on God, as a babe rests upon its mother's
> breast. It is not by great deeds, long prayers, or even
> heavy crosses that we may best give glory to God;
> self-will may taint all these, but total self-renuncia-
> tion does in truth give Him all the glory.[9]

Mrs. Herman's own words bear the same message, with the add-
ed clarifying emphasis that surrender is not a once-for-all, but a
life-long, experience:

> The central thing in prayer is not the garden of the
> soul, but the altar of dedication. If we can go to that
> altar with joy and singing, happy are we; but more
> blessed are those who ascend its steps in the naked-
> ness of faith, giving all for all and asking nothing in
> return, save that the will of God may be fulfilled
> in them.[10]

And further:

> The life of prayer is the life of conversion—a gradual,
> progressive turning from self to God. Potentially and
> ideally, that conversion is accomplished in the first
> genuine act of surrender, whereby the soul dissociates
> itself from sin and enters into a right relation with
> Eternal Love; actually it involves a lifetime of suc-
> cessive and growingly complete acts of daily self-
> denial and daily integration into Christ, a yielding up
> of the self that it may be filled with the fulness of
> God, a losing of life that it may be found again in
> Him.[11]

A little later she continues:

> It is at this point that the soul is drawn to the prayer

of intercession. . . . Prayer is seen as an apostolate, a means of making God known to others.[12]

And then she goes on to a daring assertion, which inevitably reminds us of Luther's words in his *Freedom of the Christian* about each of us being called to be a Christ for others. Mrs. Herman says:

> We feel that since Christ Himself wrought our salvation for others by a life of obedience even to the death of the Cross, so we, being joined to Him and living in union with Him, can offer our prayers, and the life behind our prayers, on behalf of others.[13]

Such a life of surrender, of oblation, to God inevitably involves discipline, both inward and outward. Nor is this only a hard and painful ordeal; rather it adds zest and meaning to our experience and even casts a strange hidden glory over life. In the light of this two-fold aspect of all spiritual discipline Mrs. Herman boldly calls us to "go into the front lines":

> There is among us an unhealthy cult of life which militates against the ideal of discipline. In our anxiety to lay due emphasis upon the positive, constructive character of Christianity, we have made a shibboleth of its doctrine of free, abundant, overflowing life, athrill with splendid vigor and indefeasible gladness. . . . We must at all costs recover the splendid spiritual courage which casts life behind its back, that puts self beneath its feet. That royal habit of soul may conceivably be created and sustained without daily discipline and mortification; but if so, we have no record of such an achievement in all the annals of sanctity.[14]

During a period of war many a man who had lived comfortably and at ease and found life a dreary, ineffectual business, suddenly discovers a well of joy and power in himself, once he endures the hard discipline of camp and fighting-line. And we may experi-

ence the same change in our spiritual life, if we would
only discard our dilettante conception of freedom
and go into the front lines with Christ.[15]

Mrs. Herman is clear, too, that sometimes and for some people the discipline requires also the renunciation of both life's
luxuries and necessities:

> The call to evangelical poverty in the specific sense
> is something entirely distinct from any social theory.
> It is the response of the loving heart to the demand
> of Christ to "sell all" and follow Him. . . . It is the
> vocation of those who offer themselves to God that
> they might express in their persons the poverty of
> Christ and so become living sacraments, as it were,
> of the Incarnation. Those who are thus called re-
> joice in sharing the common life of the poor. They do
> not frown on earthly possessions, or decry the good
> things of material life. They choose poverty, not be-
> cause they think it meritorious or good in itself, but
> because they believe that by renouncing legitimate
> comfort and being poor with Christ, they are hasten-
> ing the day when disabling poverty shall be wiped off
> the face of the earth, and all men shall share in God's
> good gifts. They are poor that they may make many
> rich.[16]

The soul that thus walks with God along these stern and
blessed ways will come to know the indescribable joys of being
gradually transformed—or suddenly transformed anew—into the
likeness of his Master. To experience even a part of these things
is indeed to "behold as in a mirror the glory of the Lord" and
to be "transformed into the same image from glory to glory."
The beginning of life in God is but a beginning. There are always further steps to be taken as we go forward in the life of
the Spirit. For although all the riches of Christ are *given* in the
initial gift of faith, often it is only much later that they are fully
received. Mrs. Herman's description of this "further-going" ex-

perience is couched in language that seems to strain to put into
human words what is really beyond words:

> Then, perhaps by a sudden sharp invasion of a new
> life . . . we become conscious of the birth of the Christ
> spirit within ourselves, and of our own birth into a
> new and wonderful world. . . . It is the world of which
> God is the center. We look upon Him, and our life is
> renewed. We are given a set of new values, a spiritual
> coinage other than that with which we have hitherto
> traded. Things that but a little while ago seemed de-
> sirable now appear as dross. . . . We discover untold
> beauties in God; we find in Christ secrets of final res-
> titution that fill us with a deathless hope. Matter is
> seen to be the storehouse of unguessed spiritual trea-
> sure, a hiding-place of holy powers, a laboratory of
> Divine alchemy. Everywhere we see mysteries of heal-
> ing and regeneration, of individual transfiguration
> and world renewal that remained hidden while self
> was our center. . . . It is as though we had developed
> a new set of faculties of appreciation and distaste,
> pleasure and pain.[17]

And this is not by any means only a solitary experience of the
soul's great joy in God. All its joys are shared, as it shares and
bears also the sorrows of others.

> At the very threshold of a sharply individual experi-
> ence, the soul that is truly submitted to God will real-
> ize its oneness with all men. It is not a question of
> cultivating the corporate feeling, as if it were some-
> thing super-added to man's experience of Christ.

> God sees us not merely as individuals, but also in an
> ideal relation to our fellows; and as the love of God
> is shed abroad in our hearts, we shall freely and gen-
> erously identify ourselves with the weakest and most
> wayward, bearing their burdens and taking them into
> the center of our prayers. . . . The soul in whose

depth Christ is truly born covets no spiritual privileges that make for isolation, refusing to be made perfect without its fellows.[18]

Such are some of the wonders of the life of prayer, the life of ever-deepening communion with God, as Mrs. Herman presents them. The quotations we have given, though not brief, are still fragmentary; but they are representative. The whole book merits thoughtful, prayerful reading. And none of us needs to be discouraged if much of what she says is still beyond us. For all of us, whatever our present stage of spiritual advancement, there are heights still to be scaled, valleys still to be traversed, flesh still to be conquered. And all of us need the shining vision ahead to stir our lagging steps.

Creative Prayer unfolds an ideal and a pattern of prayer which will both allure and guide every earnest reader on the way inward and upward. A final quotation recapitulates the teaching of the whole book:

> Prayer, in most cases, begins with personal petition. We ask benefits for ourselves and for those we love. Then we come to realize that the power of prayer lies not in the external benefit, or even in the mental and spiritual reinforcement, that comes to us through it, but in our communion with God. A new love takes possession of us, a new relationship transfigures life, a new world dawns upon our unsealed eyes. We know that communion with God does not only mean mastery over life, but that it is life itself. And as we humbly press closer to the heart of God and read a little of its secret it is gradually borne in upon us that it is only as we die to self-love that we shall be able to take our true place within the heart of love. We see that prayer is a long and arduous pilgrimage from self to God, not, indeed, the pilgrimage of those who imagine that God can be reached by human effort, but the progress of souls that have been redeemed by Christ, and now desire to be wholly found in Him.[19]

THE SETTING: 20th-century Scandinavia

THE BOOK: Basic instruction for an effective prayer life

Prayer
O. Hallesby

Prayer is the breath of the soul, by which we receive Christ into our parched and withered hearts.

Every great book of devotion is the expression and outflow of a larger spiritual movement in which the author's life was nourished, and without which the book could never have been written. This is true also of *Prayer,* by Professor Ole Hallesby of Norway. In it is distilled the essence of the life-giving movements for religious renewal that stirred all the Scandinavian lands during the 19th century. It was written only a generation ago, but its roots go back at least two hundred years more.

The Lutheran Reformation of the 16th century is one of the major landmarks in the history of Western Christendom. Luther's attack upon ecclesiastical corruption and his challenge to the external authority of the Papacy kindled flames of reform that spread swiftly, and within a generation much of northern Europe had broken away from Rome. "Justification by faith" and "the freedom of the Christian man" became the great watchwords and the controlling vision. But the victory of that evangelical vision among the masses of the people came only after a centuries-long struggle. The slowness of the process can be seen clearly illustrated in the Scandinavian countries. In name these all became Lutheran before the 16th century was over. But the churches came under the sponsorship and control of the governments, which often had more concern for outward form and organization than for the realities of spiritual life. Reading of the life of the churches and pastors in these countries during the 17th and 18th centuries can be a very disillusioning experience. The rites and records required by the state and orthodoxy of doctrine, with little relation to the life of the people, seem to have been matters of chief importance to the clergy.

But in the late 17th and 18th centuries in Lutheran Germany there arose a movement for spiritual renewal which was to have far-reaching influence within Protestantism. It came to be called "Pietism"—a name soon both beloved and derided. Like every great movement, it became the cause of division. The outstanding leader—he might even be called the founder—of the Pietist movement was Philip Jacob Spener, a pastor in Frankfort, Germany, and its basic principles were outlined in his famous book, *Pia Desideria* (Pious Goals), published in 1675. The program which Spener advocated emphasized six points. Read today, they seem not at all radical, but they really proposed a deep spiritual revolution in church life at that time. The six proposals were: 1) more extensive use of the Scriptures; 2) exercise of the priesthood of believers; 3) more stress on practice, in contrast to knowledge, of Christianity; 4) the conducting of religious controversies in a spirit of love, penitence, and prayerfulness; 5) a reform of schools and universities, with more emphasis on spiritual life; and 6) preaching for the purpose of edification. Later, among the followers of Spener, "small group meetings" for united prayer, Bible study, and mutual edification came to have an important place among their activities, and this together with other aspects of their program often became a troublesome source of controversy within the church.

Pietism was bitterly opposed and denounced, but it continued to spread. Sometimes, no doubt, it fostered undesirable practices, as false "legalism," that is, a view that the true Christian life is expressed only in following external rules and patterns. But essentially its goal was both noble and needed: the promotion and nurturing of a deeply personal Christian faith and life.

The movements of spiritual awakening in the Scandinavian countries during the 19th century were not always directly traceable to Pietist influences from Germany, but both the spirit and the aims, as well as the methods of working, were similar. In Sweden the leading publication of the movement was called *The Pietist*. In each country there arose strong spiritual leaders whose voices were heard and echoed throughout the land. C. O. Rosenius in Sweden, Paavo Ruotsalainen in Finland, Vilhelm Beck in Denmark, and Hans Nielsen Hauge in Norway were the most widely recognized leaders. All of them, and their followers, proclaimed essentially the same message: Christianity is *life*. It is not merely a doctrine or a form of church practice; it is new life in Christ. It summons men to repentance and personal faith, and to a life-style transformed from within.

In Norway the great voice denouncing formalism and calling the church to penitence and obedience to God was the peasant lay preacher, Hans Nielsen Hauge. The story of Hauge's spiritual awakening has been told and retold a thousand times in prayer houses throughout Norway and far beyond. The time was April 5, 1796, when Hauge was 25 years old, and the place his father's farm in Tune, in southern Norway. Though nurtured in a pious home and a faithful attendant at the parish church. Hauge had long been troubled by religious doubts and questions. Now on this day, as he was working in the field, he began to sing the familiar hymn beginning

> Jesus, for Thee and Thy blessed communion
> Longing possesses my heart and my mind;
> Break down all barriers that hinder our union
> Draw me to Thee, O Redeemer most kind.[1]

As he was singing the stanzas of this hymn, suddenly he found his heart set free from every burden, and filled with great joy. He has described the experience in these words:

My heart was so uplifted to God that I don't know nor
can express what took place in my soul. As soon as
my understanding returned, I regretted that I hadn't
served the loving and all-gracious God; now I felt that
no worldly thing was of importance. It was a glory
which no tongue can explain; my soul felt something
supernatural, divine, and blessed. . . . I had a completely transformed mind, a sorrow over all sins, a
burning desire that others should share the same grace.[2]

That very evening Hauge began witnessing to his new-found
faith, first of all to his two sisters, who lived at the parental home.
But soon he was speaking boldly not only to individuals but to
groups gathered in homes. Many of his hearers were immediately
brought under conviction of sin and their hearts turned to God.

Students of Hauge's life-transforming experience use various
terms to describe it, such as conversion, awakening, spiritual
breakthrough, rebirth. The important fact, however, is that what
happened to him was decisive. He was set free. He knew himself
to be a new man. And the reality of such a thoroughgoing change
became the central emphasis in his preaching. Thus Hauge's experience set a kind of basic pattern for thousands of his disciples
and followers. There is a direct line of spiritual descent from the
reborn life of Hans Nielsen Hauge to the liberated life of fellowship with God portrayed in Ole Hallesby's *Prayer*.

Within but a few months after his experience Hauge initiated
a vigorous country-wide one-man crusade of preaching and personal witness. Coworkers joined him, and before long the movement became so threatening to the church authorities that Hauge
was arrested and imprisoned. Altogether he came to spend many
hard years in prison, as a result of which his health was severely
impaired. But he was active also from prison, with both tongue
and pen. "Haugeanism" struck strong roots, and, in various
forms, has continued until our own time as a strong spiritual
force. As a result, there have been, ever since Hauge's day, two
main streams or types of spirituality in Norway, one ecclesias-

tical, liturgical, scholarly; the other informal, intensely personal, evangelistic—in a word, Haugean.

During the first half of the present century the most powerful and popular representative of Haugean Christianity in Norway was Professor Ole Hallesby—theologian, evangelist, controversial leader, voluminous author. Like Hauge, Hallesby, after years of unrest and spiritual search, passed through a personal crisis which changed him from a religious "liberal" to an ardent believer. After completing his studies, he became a professor at the Independent Theological Faculty in Oslo, where he carried out a life-long work of teaching, writing, and preaching. For a whole generation he was the acknowledged leader of "conservative Christianity" in Norway.

Concerning his book *Prayer*, Hallesby confessed, "I have had more of a desire to write this book than possibly any other that I have written. And yet I have been more afraid of this one than any other."[3] He seemed to sense that in it he was dealing with the heart of the Christian life. The little book, though written by a learned theologian, represents for us Scandinavian lay Christianity at its best. It is unpretentious in both style and content, but, like the great devotional classics of every age, it deals with essentials. Simply and directly it speaks to the awakened heart. Not only in Scandinavia, but also in America it has continued to be reprinted for nearly fifty years.

As we begin to read *Prayer*, we sense immediately that here is a book which concerns itself above all with the *individual believer*. Little attention is given to the church as a worldwide community, even less to matters of church order or organization, none at all to questions of social policy or missionary strategy. "Men are God's methods," could be written at the head of every chapter. True, there is a world-circling fellowship of prayer which is recognized and advocated, but it is not the main concern of this book. If we think of Baron von Hügel's famous definition of the three elements of religion as being the intellectual, the institutional, and the mystical, we would have to say that *Prayer* deals almost exclusively with the mystical element, the

realm of the soul when the closet door has been shut, and a
person is alone with God.

Prayer begins with Christ's words in the third chapter of Revelation: "Behold, I stand at the door and knock: if any man hear
my voice and open the door I will come in to him, and will sup
with him, and he with me." No passage in the whole Bible, says
the author, throws more light on prayer than this one. For it
shows that it is not we, but God, who initiates prayer. "Before
they call, I will answer," says the prophet." [4] Prayer is not a
matter of following any complicated or well thought-out program.
It does not depend on human effort or exertion, but simply on
our willingness to "open the door."

Paradoxical as it may seem, effectiveness in prayer grows out
of a sense of *helplessness* on our part. Prayer is the breath of the
soul. As the air surrounds our bodies on every side, so the grace
and blessing of God encompass us, ready to enter every receptive
heart. The Israelites bitten by serpents in the wilderness needed
but to look, and there was healing. The child at its mother's
breast has no words, nor even formulated thoughts, yet its
"prayer" for food and care is heard and answered. When the
sinner acknowledges his own utter helplessness, this very fact
creates in him the humble, broken heart to which the Lord can
truly minister.

> Helplessness is the decisive factor, not only in our
> prayer life, but in our whole relationship to God. As
> long as we are conscious of our helplessness, . . . we
> will expect nothing of ourselves and therefore bring
> all our difficulties and hindrances to God in prayer.[5]

Only after such a very strong emphasis upon our utter de-
pendence and helplessness does Professor Hallesby go on to point
out the other crucial element in prayer, namely *faith*. And this
too he defines with disarming simplicity. Faith is not a state of
mind or heart which we must "work up," as it were. Rather, it
is simply *coming* to God in our need.

You have more faith than you think you have. You

have faith enough to pray; you have faith enough to believe that you will be heard.[6]

I need not exert myself and try to force myself to believe or try to chase doubt out of my heart. Both are equally useless . . . [I need] only to tell Jesus how weak my faith is. I have let Jesus into my heart. And he will fulfill my heart's desire.[7]

Against this fundamental background of prayer as an intensely personal relation between the soul and God, Hallesby goes on to discuss the various aspects of the prayer life, its problems and its power, its struggles, its defeats, and its victories. Important sections of the book are concerned with prayer as *work*, as the instrument of our cooperation with God for his kingdom.

Whenever we touch His almighty arm, some of his omnipotence streams in upon us, into our souls and into our bodies. And not only that, but, through us, it streams to others. . . . This power is entirely independent of time and space. . . . Here is an example of wireless transmission of power, which transcends the dreams of the boldest inventor.[8]

The vital work of intercession should be carried on not only for the great masses and movements of mankind, and for the church both at home and abroad, but it should be directed also on behalf of certain definite individuals. "Ask the Spirit of prayer," says Dr. Hallesby, "to assign to you the individuals for whom you should pray." [9]

The work of praying is prerequisite to all other work in the Kingdom of God, for the simple reason that it is by prayer that we couple the powers of heaven to our helplessness . . . the powers which can capture strongholds and make the impossible possible.[10]

Such a work of intercession needs and deserves careful planning and an ordered program for the prayer chamber. For most of us this can be helped by the keeping of a "prayer list." Dr. Hallesby speaks slightingly of most printed prayer books, but personally written prayer books he highly commends. And he recognizes that occasional lapses of memory or practice do not by any means invalidate the prayer program as such. He discusses at length, and evidently on the basis of personal experience, what a struggle it can be actually to enter regularly into the work of prayer. Satan and our own flesh are ever at hand to tempt and to disturb. But victory is possible, where "the peace of God guards our hearts." [11] Intense activity, far-soaring thought, well-formulated sentences are not at all necessary in prayer. The most important thing is just to be in the divine presence. There our own hearts are searched and cleansed and healed. And through us there can flow a healing stream to others.

Other problems of the prayer life are also effectively dealt with in this book: the relation between obedience and prayer, the meaning of unanswered prayer, the place of fasting in the prayer life, prayer and physical healing, the relation between intercessory prayer and the divine omnipotence, the prayers of the unconverted. In each instance the teaching is uncomplicated, clear, often helpful and convincing. The whole Christian life, and the prayer life, are presented in the spirit of Christ's words, "Unless you turn and become like children, you will never enter the kingdom of heaven." [12] This high commendation of simplicity will be an offense to some readers. But again and again, beneath the unadorned and childlike words lie hidden treasures of great wisdom.

Appropriately, the final chapter deals with the work of the Holy Spirit, who is both the source and the sustainer of a true life of prayer. The Holy Spirit must be the Companion and Teacher of all who would walk with Christ. Therefore the most basic and important of all our prayers is the prayer for the Holy Spirit. And Christ has assured us that the Father will give him, the best of all gifts, to everyone who prays for his coming. Then in truth we shall be girded for the work of God among men.

Such childlike petitions for the Spirit of prayer will little by little bring about a change in our prayer life which we hardly thought possible. Without noticing it ourselves, prayer will become the great unifying factor in our distracted and busy lives. . . . A longing to talk with God about everything will arise. Everything we see and hear in connection with our dear ones, our friends, our enemies . . . temporal and spiritual affairs, small things and great, the hard and the easy, all the observations and experiences which fill and shape our daily lives, will naturally and readily begin to take the form of prayer. . . . The Spirit of prayer makes us so intimate with God that we scarcely pass through an experience before we speak to Him about it.[13]

And the angels on the prayer ladder raised to heaven go both up and down. Professor Hallesby uses a different figure to convey the same truth:

The longer you live this kind of life, the more answers to prayer you will experience. As white snowflakes falling quietly and thickly on a winter day, answers to prayer will settle down upon you every step you take, even to your dying day. . . . This shower of answers to prayer will continue to your dying hour, nor will it cease then.[14]

The heritage of Pietism came to a significant flowering in the "awakening" movements in 19th-century Scandinavia. In all four countries the message proclaimed was clear and strong: Christianity is to be personally experienced, and the individual set free into a trustful, responsible fellowship with God. It is this message which is presupposed on every page of Hallesby's *Prayer*. For only a justified, liberated heart can experience intimate, childlike prayer life such as he describes. It is in this sense that *Prayer* is a "pietistic" book.

This type of "lay Christianity" has often been despised by the worldly-wise, at times also in the church. And it does have its weaknesses, such as a certain narrowness of outlook and, frequently, a lack of stress upon the larger world-wide Christian community. But granted such weaknesses, few spiritual lighthouses of Christendom are more dependable guides than lives of evangelical prayer.

At the same time, it is important to remember that other concepts of the prayer life are by no means on a lower level. Christians of widely varying persuasions and patterns have known and written of the blessedness of the "interior castle." The house of prayer has many mansions. The subtle self-analyses of St. Augustine and the prophetic social vision of John Woolman have their place as truly as Dr. Hallesby's unsophisticated language of the heart. In the church there is room for both activists and pietists, for both philosophers and peasants, for both high churchmen and unschooled laymen, to kneel together.

THE SETTING: 20th-century England

THE BOOK: Meditations on the Christian Creed and the inner life

The School of Charity
Evelyn Underhill

The Christian Creed is a handlist of the soul's essential requirements: the iron ration of truths, the knowledge of mighty realities, which rightly used is sufficient to feed and safeguard our supernatural life throughout its course.

To begin to read Evelyn Underhill's *The School of Charity* is like rounding a curve on a mountain drive, and suddenly coming upon a breathtaking view of far-stretching valleys and mountain heights. For this volume of meditations on the Nicene Creed, by one of the truly great religious writers of our time, combines a remarkable depth of thought, beauty of style, and sweeping spiritual perspective. To some it may at first seem difficult reading, but if it is read thoughtfully and in not too large segments at a time, it will yield rewarding spiritual insight. For, in a sense, *The School of Charity* may be said to resemble *The Confessions of St. Augustine*—an almost inexhaustible source of both Scripture-grounded instruction and spiritual inspiration.

As in the case of many of the spiritual classics, *The School of Charity* is a fruit of the life and experience of its author. The long road from doubt to faith which she traveled is reflected again and again in her treatment of many difficult questions which beset the Christian's thought in our time. To gain some knowledge of Evelyn Underhill's life is therefore perhaps the best preparation for sharing her high vision of the life in Christ.

Born in 1875, Evelyn Underhill was the daughter of a distinguished London barrister. Her childhood home was thoroughly secularized. (She has described it in a terse sentence: "I wasn't brought up to religion.") [1] In it, however, she absorbed fundamental moral ideals, so that even as a young girl she made a long list of her faults and shortcomings. But it was only after many years of serious thought, and a brilliant educational career at King's College, London, that she was gradually led to belief in God and to a full Christian faith. Years of earnest quest and discipline were spent under the tutelage of the greatest thinkers and the greatest saints of the Christian past. Many of these writers she discovered early, and their teachings were slowly absorbed into her experience and her writings.

It was through her first "great" book, *Mysticism* (1911), that she achieved recognition as one of the outstanding religious writers of her time. As her outlook broadened with the years, she wrote in many fields: fiction, theology, philosophy, education, poetry, letters of spiritual counsel. All of these reflected and recorded her deepening development in thought and life. In *Mysticism,* her convictions seem not yet to be fully Christ-centered. But about the time of its publication, she came to know a great teacher and friend, the eminent Roman Catholic theologian, Baron Friedrich von Hügel, whose influence was to be decisive in her whole subsequent life. She herself never became a Catholic, but von Hügel's thought, even after his death in 1925, remained a guiding star for both her life and her thinking.

Revealing how long were the years of her spiritual quest, as late as 1927 she writes of herself:

> Until about five years ago I never had *any* personal experience of our Lord . . . I was a convinced Theocentric, . . . I had, from time to time, what seemed to be vivid experiences of God, from the time of my

conversion from agnosticism (about 20 years ago now) . . . I went to the Baron. . . . Somehow by his prayers or something he *compelled* me to experience Christ. . . . The New Testament, which once I couldn't make much of, or meditate on, now seems full of things I never noticed.[2]

The School of Charity, written a few years later, shows how far her convictions had by that time been transformed.

Evelyn Underhill was a scholar and thinker of the highest order. Her books deal profoundly with the whole field of Christian spirituality—its intellectual basis, its liturgical expression, its history in the lives of the saints, its daily application in present experience. Her scholarly achievement was given notable recognition by her being awarded an honorary Doctorate in Divinity by Kings College. Yet as she pursued these ways of far-ranging study and inward discipline, her personal life was not isolated from ordinary human experience. She loved the country— the trees, the flowers, the birds, the little animals; she traveled often; after her marriage in 1907 she kept her evenings, aside from special duties, for her husband at home; she cultivated close personal friendships; for a long period she spent two afternoons a week among the poor in the slums and near-slums of London. Her life was shaped from without as well as from within. No one believed more completely in the principle of incarnation than did she—the spirit must clothe itself with flesh in every area of life. Concerning the total impact of her life, Charles Williams, a devoted friend and the editor of her *Letters,* has written:

> Her vocation was rather to be . . . in the end, a light. The light might, and certainly did, illuminate and guide, but first it merely shone.[3]

The light that shines through *The School of Charity* is, above all, that of a beautiful life found by Christ after long seeking, and then lived out in him.

In harmony with the author's own experience of a parallel development of her inner life and her full acceptance of a Christ-centered faith, *The School of Charity* directs us to both an inward pilgrimage of prayer and discipleship and an ever-deepening faith, centered in the Incarnate Christ.

At the very heart of the Christian faith is the doctrine that the Word became flesh. But this is not an isolated article in the Creed; it is integral with our whole faith in the Triune God, indeed with our view of all Reality. The vision of God, however, too splendid for our human eyes, can truly come to us only as reflected in the humility of the Incarnate One and only as we see it from "within"—with eyes and heart that have been cleansed by prayer. Miss Underhill uses a familiar example, giving it a beautiful twofold interpretation:

> It sometimes happens that one goes to see a cathedral which is famous for the splendor of its glass; only to discover that, seen outside, the windows give us no hint whatever of that which awaits us within. They all look alike; dull, thick, and grubby. . . . Then we open the door and go inside . . . and at once we are surrounded by a radiance, a beauty, that lie beyond the fringe of speech. The universal Light of God in which we live and move, and yet which in its reality always escapes us, pours through those windows . . . and shows us things of which we never dreamed before.
>
> In the same way, the deep mysteries of the Being of God . . . cannot be seen by us, until they have passed through a human medium, a human life. Nor can that life, and all that it means as a revelation of God, his eternal truth and beauty, be realized by us from the outside. . . . It is only within the place of prayer, recollection, worship and love . . . that we can cleanse our vision . . . and fully and truly receive the revelation of Reality which is made to us in Christ. . . .
>
> For here, a Light we can bear to look at . . . comes to us from a Light we cannot bear to look at even whilst

we worship it. . . . What we see is not very sensa-
tional. . . . First we see a baby, and a long hidden
growth; and then the unmeasured outpouring and self
spending of an other-worldly love and mercy; teaching, healing, rescuing and transforming, but never
trying to get anything for itself; . . . consummated at
last in the most generous and lonely of deaths, issuing
in a victory which has given life ever since to men's
souls.[4]

The Incarnation, both as the perfect revelation of the heart
of God and as the perfect pattern for every Christ-ed human
life, continued to unfold throughout the whole earthly life of
our Lord:

We see the new life growing in secret. . . . We see the
child in the carpenter's workshop. He does not go outside the frame of the homely life in which he ap-
peared. It did quite well for him, and will do quite
well for us. There is no need for peculiar conditions
in order to grow in the spiritual life. . . . The third-
rate little town among the hills . . . reproves us when
we begin to fuss about our opportunities and our
scope. And this quality of quietness, ordinariness,
simplicity, with which the saving action of God enters
history, endures from the beginning to the end.[5]

Nor was this revelation of Incarnate Love among the routine
scenes of human life broken off even by the shattering experience of the Passion and the Cross. After the Easter triumph it
continued on the same level, giving of itself amidst common and
everyday surroundings, reaffirming the pattern for the lives of
all who would follow in his steps:

The [resurrected] glory of the Divine Humanity is not
shown in the Temple and the Synagogue. He seeks out
his nervous followers within the arena of ordinary
life; meets them behind the locked doors of the Upper
Room, waits for them in the early morning by the

lakeside, walks with them on the country road, and
suddenly discloses himself in the breaking of bread.
The characters of the old life which are carried
through into this new and glorified life are just those
which express a homely and cherishing love.[6]

And so it must be, says Evelyn Underhill, in every true Christian life:

> The real mark of spiritual triumph—the possession of
> that more lovely, more abundant life which we dis-
> cern in moments of deep prayer—is not an abstraction
> from this world, but a return to it; a willing use of its
> conditions as material for the expression of love.
> There is nothing high-minded about Christian holi-
> ness. It is most at home in the slum, the street, the
> hospital ward. . . . A little water, some fragments of
> bread, and a chalice of wine are enough to close the
> gap between two worlds, and give the soul and senses
> a trembling contact with the Eternal Charity. By
> means of these its creatures, that touch still cleanses,
> and that hand still feeds.[7]

In addition to its being so intimately an outgrowth of the author's own life experience, we may mention three other elements
in the content of *The School of Charity* which contribute to its
uniquely helpful character as a spiritual guide: 1) its solid basis
in the Christian Creed; 2) its constant reference to the great
devotional writings of the past; and 3) its complete church-
centeredness.

As to the first of these elements, we have already spoken of its
illuminating portrayal of the Incarnation. But for Evelyn Underhill, the entire Creed is both a treasury of biblical truth and
a "handlist of the soul's essential requirements." The most basic
equipment for the Christian's journey through life, she says, is
not a set of rules or methods, but rather a deepened understanding of the foundations of his faith. She calls upon her readers,
therefore, as a salutary lenten exercise (the book was originally

written for Lent) to make a careful reexamination of the various
elements in that equipment.

> Lent is a good moment for such spiritual stocktaking;
> a pause, a retreat from life's busy surface to its solemn
> deeps. There we can consider our possessions; and dis-
> criminate between the necessary stores which have
> been issued to us, and must be treasured and kept in
> good order, and the odds and ends which we have ac-
> cumulated for ourselves.[8]

To undertake such a spiritual stocktaking, to ask yourself,
step by step, what you really believe on this or that point, requires courage. But it is a very profitable exercise, and anyone
who has tried it can testify to its bracing effect on the soul. To
examine, under Evelyn Underhill's guidance, the enduring realities of revelation and experience which sustain our convictions
concerning the spiritual world in which we live and move, is
indeed to be led forth anew into paths of deepened faith and
righteousness.

Securely built upon the Christian Creed, *The School of Charity* also draws, constantly and widely, upon the riches of other
devotional writings from all the churches, East and West, Protestant, Catholic, and Orthodox. Evelyn Underhill was at home
in all the Christian traditions, and learned freely and gratefully
from them all. Her writings are replete with references to the
lives and the teachings of the saintly men and women of other
generations, calling us to heed their words and follow in their
steps.

> The Power that desires to fill and use us, is the Power
> that filled and used Paul and Augustine, Benedict,
> Bruno and Bernard, Francis of Assisi and Catherine
> of Siena, Fox and Wesley . . . that went to the ends of
> the earth with Francis Xavier and Henry Martyn,
> or transformed a narrow sphere in Father Wainwright
> and the Cure d'Ars. . . . We are "called to be saints"
> —self-emptied vessels of the Holy—not for our own
> sake but for the sake of the world. . . . In the world

of spirit, that which is done by one is done for all
since the real actor is the Charity of God.[9]

For Evelyn Underhill the Communion of Saints was a basic
reality undergirding the whole Christian experience. She herself lived in the truth proclaimed in her words: "Entering the
mighty current of living Charity, means entering into a real
communion with other souls, who are linked to us within
that tide." [10]

Closely related to this basic conviction is the fact that the
spirituality of *The School of Charity* is completely church-centered. Evelyn Underhill taught no individualistic Christianity.
Nor did she advocate merely a broad and "spiritualized" pattern of Christian community. Her faith and her spirituality
were both Christ-centered and church-centered. Reverently it
may be said of her too that she "loved the church and gave herself up for her." She believed in the actually existing church,
not some idealized conception of it, the church with all its
shortcomings and sins. She loved the history of the church, its
art and its architecture, its literature, its music and its hymns,
but she also loved and served the church in its *present reality,*
with all its temporal "spots and wrinkles," as the bearer of salvation to souls and to nations. From this "everyday" church,
she insists, none of us is permitted to shy away, in order to seek
and follow, some more exalted vision.

> When we think of pews and hassocks and the Parish
> Magazine, we tend to rebel against the yoke of offi-
> cial religion, with its suggestions of formalism and
> even frowsiness. It seems far too stiff and institutional,
> too unventilated to represent the generous and life-
> giving dealings of the Divine Charity with men. . . .
> [But] the whole Body is the Bride of Christ, a body,
> as St. Paul says, having many different members, some
> of a very odd shape, some of a very lowly kind. And it
> is in this Body, at once mysterious and homely, that
> the individual Christian must consent to sink his life,
> in order that he may find true life.[11]

For this "homely" church is also the glorious and exalted "One Holy Catholic Church" encompassing all the world and all the ages, both the object of our faith and the habitation of God, where our troubled minds and hearts find rest.

It is "the mystery of God," hidden indeed through ages past, but now revealed as the divinely planned living temple, in which Jew and Gentile, all mankind, may find freedom, love, and life everlasting.

Among the many beautiful corollaries of such a view of the church, *The School of Charity* gives special stress to its importance for the prayer life. No Christian prays alone; even in the innermost closet he is a living part of the Body of Christ, through which the Holy Spirit intercedes for all, also when we know not how to pray as we ought and can only breathe in groanings that cannot be uttered. Here are Evelyn Underhill's words concerning the organic character of all true prayer:

> Because of this deep fact of the Living Church, this interconnection of all surrendered spirits, the prayer of one unit can avail for all. We pray as an organism, not as a mere crowd of souls; . . . "I believe in the Holy Catholic Church, the Communion of Saints," says the Apostles' Creed. . . . Here that rich New Testament word "Communion" bears a double reference. For on one hand it means that we believe in the whole fellowship, the society of saints, known and unknown, living and dead, their reality and power, their aliveness, their authority, their witness to the facts of the spiritual life; and on the other hand that we believe there is a true communion, a genuine sharing between all the members of the one Body. Within its universal prayer thinker and lover, sufferer and worker, Catholic and Quaker, pool their resources.[12]

Such a vision of the larger meaning of prayer cannot fail to give new depth and new joy to even our poorest attempts at petition and intercession.

It is not strange that with such a view of Christian community and the life of prayer, Evelyn Underhill gave much of her time and strength to conducting spiritual retreats. *The School of Charity* is dedicated "To Pleshey, with my love." Pleshey was her favorite retreat-house, where she often ministered, especially during the later years of her life.

Her final chapter, entitled "The World to Come" lifts our eyes to the everlasting hills of Christian hope. This hope, she says, has two intertwining aspects. On the one hand, it rests its sure confidence in the reality of the world beyond, where not only will tears be wiped away, but where perfections dimly seen but passionately longed for in our present life will stand forth in all their splendor:

> The pure joy of a keen unbaffled intelligence, of an
> unhindered vision of beauty; ears that can hear what
> the universe is always trying to say to us, hearts at
> last capable of a pure and unlimited love.[13]

All that we call the "physical" world will be transformed. Our limited spectrum of color and our narrow scale of sound are "mere chunks cut out of a world of infinite color and sound —the world that is drawing near, charged with the unbearable splendor and music of the Absolute God." [14]

But the other aspect of our hope is equally important: this unseen world must even now be made more and more the controling reality in our present world that is "seen." This phase of our hope is the insistent challenge to the church and to the Christian: the Body of Christ exists to work for the world's transformation, to bring Eternal Life into time. And this is to be done, not in some isolated setting of quiet peace and beauty, but "with the clock ticking, the engagement-book bristling, . . . and every new edition of the paper recording some new movement, new sin, new sorrow of the restless world." [15] It is here that we are to find and live that "eternal life which consists in the disclosure of the Divine Charity." [16]

The fullness of the thought of *The School of Charity,* encompassing and interpreting the whole historic Creed and applying it to the many facets of the Christian's life and experience, cannot be presented in summary form or merely by excerpted quotation. Evelyn Underhill's own words deserve to be read and pondered, for her teaching makes the Creed come alive. Father and Son, Creator and Lord, Spirit and Church—each name and word, touched and illumined by her interpretation, takes on new meaning, awakens new gratitude, summons to renewed praise and thanksgiving. Best of all, as we take up, time after time, our task of spiritual stocktaking, we not only gain new insight, but are girded with new strength through a renewed vision of the One God in whom all the thought and all the counsel of *The School of Charity* are centered.

THE SETTING: 20th-century Germany

THE BOOK: Prerequisites and patterns of
                Christian community living

Life Together
Dietrich Bonhoeffer

*Even when sin and misunderstanding burden the
communal life, is not the sinning brother still a
brother? . . . Will not his sin be a constant occasion for me to give thanks that both of us may live
in the forgiving love of God in Jesus Christ?*

Dietrich Bonhoeffer died as a martyr in Nazi Germany in 1945—a political martyr for plotting against Hitler's
regime, and a martyr for Jesus Christ, in obedience to whom he
took up the cross of resistance even when he knew it would
probably mean death. Today, throughout the whole Christian
world, his name and memory are held in highest honor. Few
men are more frequently quoted both in scholarly theological
circles and among the rank and file of lay Christians. His heroic
example and his liberating writings alike speak with convicting
and convincing power.

Bonhoeffer was born in Breslau, in what is now Poland, in
1906, the sixth child in a family of eight. The family moved to
Berlin, when the father, a noted physician, accepted a call to become the first professor of psychiatry at the University there. All
the Bonhoeffer children grew up with academic interests, and
by the time Dietrich was sixteen he had decided to study theology. He took his doctorate at twenty-one. For a time he was a

pastor in Barcelona, and later in London. Then, after a year as a student in Union Seminary, New York, he was a lecturer at the University of Berlin for about five years.

By this time the clouds of the Hitler period were deepening, and he was forced out of his university position. Totally opposed to Hitler's "German Christian" program, he worked for the Confessing Church and for the Resistance. In 1937 he was appointed director of an "underground seminary" which moved from place to place within Germany. It was his life there, in close fellowship with a group of 23 theological students, that led to the writing of *Life Together*.

Under English and American influences, Bonhoeffer had almost become a pacifist. But the situation of persecution and tyranny prevailing in his native land brought him to the conviction that a Christian must also take his part as a citizen in this world, even when it means engaging in physical violence. Dr. John W. Doberstein, the translator of *Life Together,* gives this clarifying statement of Bonhoeffer's convictions in relation to this crucial question:

> For him Christianity could never be merely intellectual theory, doctrine divorced from life, or mystical emotion, but always it must be responsible, obedient action, the discipleship of Christ in every situation of concrete everyday life, personal and public. And it was this that led him in the end to prison and death.[1]

The Gestapo suspected and followed him. In April, 1943, together with a brother-in-law and others, he was arrested. He spent two years as a prisoner, toward the end moved from one prison to another. Finally, at the special order of Heinrich Himmler, he was condemned to death and hanged in Flossenburg Prison on April 9, 1945—just before its liberation by American troops. Eight years earlier he had written: "When Christ calls a man, he bids him come and die." [2]

A fellow-prisoner at the end, an English officer named Payne Best, has left this testimony concerning Bonhoeffer's last days:

He seemed always to spread an atmosphere of happiness, and joy over the least incident and profound gratitude for the mere fact that he was alive. . . . He was one of the very few persons I have ever met for whom God was real and always near. . . . On Sunday, April 8, 1945, Pastor Bonhoeffer conducted a little service of worship and spoke to us in a way that went to the heart of all of us.[3]

Bonhoeffer's farewell words to Payne Best were: "This is the end, but for me it is the beginning of life." [4] The text for his sermon on that last Sunday had been, "By his stripes we are healed."

Such was Dietrich Bonhoeffer's noble life—and death. There is abundance of witness that in all the turmoil and struggle of the last years, his warm and personal faith in Christ remained unbroken. His biographer and close friend, Eberhard Bethge, has written:

He was willing to take such risks for civil rights as to engage in conspiracy, and yet he did not simply leave behind him the devotional practice of a long life.[5]

Many of his letters sent from prison bear witness to a warm and victorious faith. In the words of a devout Roman Catholic reader of those published letters, they are marked by a spirit of "genuine unforced piety" and seemed to be "founded on devotion and trusting optimism." [6]

Nevertheless, the publication of Bonhoeffer's *Letters and Papers from Prison* aroused storms of discussion and disagreement as to what his theological views actually were. Especially certain recurring expressions, such as "non-religious Christianity," "a world come of age," and "Jesus, the man for others" raised questions in the minds of many who wondered whether the great theologian, under the pressure of bitter circumstances and the cruelties and absurdities of human existence, had actually given up his evangelical faith. The intricate arguments pro and con do not concern us here. We mention those persistent question-ings only to show that even the most devoted faith can sometimes have to pass through seasons of deep intellectual and spiritual struggle. In and out of prison, Dietrich Bonhoeffer was striving to find an uncompromisingly honest understanding of life and its realities. The details of his theological views may never be finally and fully explained. But the witness of his heroic, faith-filled life and death shines on, "a burning and shining light" amid all the darkness of our century.

During the time that Bonhoeffer was in charge of the "emergency seminary" in Pomerania, he wrote two books of vigorous Christian witness rejecting all compromise in the church struggle then taking place in Germany: *The Cost of Discipleship* (1937), and *Life Together* (1938). *Life Together* has a particular freshness of appeal for us, even in our very different situation, because its basic theme is an aspect of spirituality often neglected, namely, the meaning and practice of Christian community. In the church today there is, it is true, much emphasis on the Christian's duties and responsibilities in society. But the distinctiveness of Bonhoeffer's book is that it sets forth so clearly that true community is achieved only in Christ, and it gives wise and pointed instruction regarding the spirit and methods whereby this community comes into being. Completely practical in its approach, it is less a book to be read and meditated upon than a book to be studied and obeyed. Taking its stand clearly on the Word, the revelation in Christ, it faces one by one the major problems of Christians living together, and points out the resources available for building true Christian community.

In the close-knit fellowship of the "underground seminary" the faults and shortcomings of the individual students—and of their leader—came into clear focus. Bonhoeffer's discussion of these problems and their solutions in a life of Christ-centered fellowship is often startlingly frank.

At times, too, we may feel that his prescriptions for living the spiritual life are too rigorous, too structured, too much the product of an orderly "German" mind. But most of Christian life today errs far more in the opposite direction: we tend to be careless, easy-going, undisciplined. So even if we cannot follow his instructions in all details, Bonhoeffer's words of counsel and direction deserve to be carefully weighed. They originate in life and are aimed to shape life. Certainly, if heeded, they will inject some "iron atoms" into our flabby souls.

He speaks first of three aspects of nurturing Christian community: being together, praying together, and eating together. Concerning the privilege of having the physical nearness of other Christians, we can discern a tragic sadness underlying his words when we remember the years he spent alone in prison:

> The physical presence of other Christians is a source of incomparable joy and strength to the believer. Longingly, the imprisoned Apostle Paul calls his "dearly beloved son in the faith," Timothy, to come to him in prison in the last days of his life; he would see him again and have him near. . . . Remembering the congregation in Thessalonica, Paul prays "night and day . . . exceedingly that we might see your face."

> The believer feels no shame, as though he were still living too much in the flesh, when he yearns for the physical presence of other Christians. Man was created in a body, the Son of God appeared on earth in a body, he was raised in a body, in the sacrament the believer receives the Lord Christ in the body, and the resurrection of the dead will bring about the perfected fellowship of God's spiritual-physical creatures.[7]

Bonhoeffer has much to say about prayer, both private and among our brothers. Like the other masters of the spiritual life, he knows that prayer is the heart of religion. United praying, in the home and in the church fellowship, is to be both spoken and sung—for singing, too, has a large place in the Christian life. And for the individual and in the congregation "the Psalter is the great school of prayer."[8] Prayers may often be formal or liturgical, but by no means always. Concerning the value and importance of free prayer as an aid to Christian community, Bonhoeffer writes:

> No matter what objections there may be, the fact sim-
> ply remains that where Christians want to live togeth-
> er under the Word of God, they may and they should
> pray together in their own words. They have com-
> mon petitions, common thanks, common interces-
> sions to bring to God, and they should do so joy-
> fully and confidently. . . . It is in fact the most normal
> thing in the common Christian life to pray together.
> Good and profitable as our restraints may be in order
> to keep our prayer pure and biblical, they must
> nevertheless not stifle free prayer itself, for Jesus
> Christ attached a great promise to it.[9]

Our daily meals together, too, should be a means of building Christian community. Every meal, says Bonhoeffer, should have a certain likeness to the Holy Sacrament, in which the presence of Christ is manifested. Every meal, too, should have a certain festive quality about it, for through our daily meals God is calling us to rejoice and be glad. This becomes the more true when we remember that daily bread is always "our," never "my" daily bread.

> We share our bread. Thus we are firmly bound to
> one another, not only in the Spirit but in our whole
> physical being. . . . "Deal thy bread to the hungry . . ."
> (Isa. 58:7). So long as we eat our bread together we
> shall have sufficient even with the least.[10]

> The Scriptures speak of three kinds of table fellow-
> ship that Jesus keeps with his own: daily fellowship
> at table, the table fellowship of the Lord's Supper,
> and the final table fellowship in the Kingdom of God.
> But in all three the one thing that counts is that
> "their eyes were opened and they knew him." [11]

The Christian, to grow strong and effective, must have not

only companionship and nourishment but also discipline. Like all the great spiritual teachers, Bonhoeffer lays great emphasis on this aspect of the Christian life. Among its most important forms he stresses three: the cultivation of silence, the control of the tongue, and the confession of sins.

Spiritual silence is defined as "the simple stillness of the individual under the Word of God." [12] By this Bonhoeffer means not only a quiet listening to the voice of God in church or in Scripture reading, but also keen attention to "the Word within":

> We are silent at the beginning of the day because God should have the first word, and we are silent before going to sleep because the last word also belongs to God. We keep silence solely for the sake of the Word. . . .
>
> This stillness before the Word will exert its influence upon the whole day.[13]

But if our silences are important, the control of our speech is equally so. We must learn to speak so that our words "may minister grace unto the hearers" (Ephesians 4:29). And the right exercise of speech will be a strong creative force for the building of true community.

> He who holds his tongue in check controls both mind and body (James 3:2ff). Thus it must be a decisive rule of every Christian fellowship that each individual is prohibited from saying much that occurs to him. . . .
>
> Where the discipline of the tongue is practiced . . . each individual will make a matchless discovery. He will be able to cease from constantly scrutinizing the other person, condemning him, putting him in his particular place. . . . Now we can allow the brother to exist as a completely free person, as God made him to be.[14]

One of the most effective aids toward achieving "breakthrough into community" is the confession of sins. Both secular

and Christian counselors have known and stressed the value of
sharing guilt through confession if burdened hearts are to be
set free. But it is, says Bonhoeffer, supremely in the Christian
community, the Christian congregation, that this can and should
occur.

> In confession the break-through to community takes
> place. Sin demands to have a man by himself. It
> withdraws him from the community. The more iso-
> lated a person is, the more destructive will be the
> power of sin over him. . . . Sin wants to remain un-
> known. It shuns the light. In the darkness of the
> unexpressed it poisons the whole being of a person.
> This can happen even in the midst of a pious com-
> munity. In confession, the light of the Gospel breaks
> into the darkness and seclusion of the heart. . . .
>
> Since the confession of sin is made in the presence of
> a Christian brother, the last stronghold of self-justi-
> fication is abandoned.[15]

Without confession the Christian is deprived of one of his
greatest resources and soon his life will wither and die. But
through confession comes a "break-through into joy."

> As the first disciples left all and followed when Jesus
> called, so in confession the Christian gives up all and
> follows. Confession is discipleship. Life with Jesus
> Christ and his community has begun. . . . What hap-
> pened to us in baptism is bestowed upon us anew
> in confession. We are delivered out of darkness into
> the Kingdom of Jesus Christ. . . . "Weeping may en-
> dure for the night, but joy cometh in the morning."
> (Ps. 30:5).[16]

And finally, says Bonhoeffer:

> Though it is true that confession is an act in the
> name of Christ that is complete in itself . . . it serves
> the Christian community especially as a preparation

for the common reception of the holy Communion.
Reconciled to God and men, Christians desire to receive the body and blood of Christ . . . and receiving
that [they receive] forgiveness, new life, and salvation. . . . The fellowship of the Lord's Supper is the
superlative fulfillment of Christian fellowship.[17]

The pathway of discipleship may at times be a very difficult
one: "The gate is narrow and the way is hard." [18] But it is supremely a way of joy, of joy unspeakable in the community
which only Christ through his Holy Spirit can create.

Long ago the Church Father Tertullian said, "The blood of
the martyrs is the seed of the Church." *Life Together* is a precious seed left by one of the great Christian martyrs of our
time. Its vision of Christian truth and practice, was, in a sense,
purchased at the cost of the lifeblood of its heroic author. We
who read it today are his unworthy debtors—and his would-be
disciples. We are called to walk in his way, though we may never
follow it to the end, as he did.

Epilog

Like the householder in our Lord's parable, we who have walked together on the inward pilgrimage, illumined by some of the great spiritual classics, have found treasures both new and old. Some of these treasures may have seemed obscure and difficult to obtain, but some were transparently clear and so precious that our hearts were stirred to "sell all" and immediately buy the field where they lay.

But the living of the spiritual life is not the decision of a moment; it is the achievement of a lifetime, enabled and empowered by the Holy Spirit. Each heart must possess its own possessions. Things new and old must alike be recognized, examined, weighed; only "bit by bit" do they become a part of the soul's personal patrimony.

As all the spiritual classics stress, the heart of this process of spiritual growth is *prayer*. And though the costs of a dedicated life of prayer are great, the rewards are beyond measure.

Of these rewards the first and ultimate is the experience of a deepening communion with God himself—the sense of his presence, his strength-giving grace, his unfailing love. "Whom have I in heaven but thee? And there is nothing upon earth that I desire besides thee," cries the psalmist who has won his way through deep doubt to the assurance of unbroken fellowship with the Eternal. "My flesh and my heart may fail, but God is the strength of my heart and my portion forever." [1]

And almost as wonderful as the nearness of God is the vivid sense of an encompassing fellowship of those, from all the Christian ages, who have lived and wrought as good friends of God. In the spiritual classics, the whole company of these seem to draw near, from every clime and communion, until we are surrounded by a great cloud of "the spirits of just men made perfect." Within this goodly fellowship we share the crust of the Desert Fathers; we laugh and sing with St. Francis and his Little Poor Men; with Martin Luther we glory in the freedom of the justified Christian; with John Woolman we bear the burdens of poverty and slavery; with Brother Lawrence in his kitchen we meet God among the pots and kettles. The riches of all are ours, and we are Christ's and Christ is God's.

Yet our final goal can never be our own spiritual enrichment or enjoyment. The great spiritual writers all clearly teach that the coming of the Kingdom takes priority over the attainment of even the finest of our individual aims. Life for each Christian is to be found, not by saving and perfecting it, but by losing it on behalf of the Kingdom. The coming of that Kingdom in its fulness, not only within our own hearts but in the whole world and through the whole church—the Holy City coming down out of heaven from God—must be the constant theme of both our prayer and our living.

"Even so, come, Lord Jesus," prays the Bride at the close of the Book of Revelation. So the Church has prayed through two thousand years, and yet the full coming of the Kingdom tarries. But thank God, it is not only the Bride that prays for the coming and the consummation. Also *the Spirit* says, "Come!"

Therein lies our true hope: a new revelation of the voice and the power of the Holy Spirit, calling, uniting, perfecting the people of God. Many signs across the world today signal a deep and widespread renewal, a new fulness of the Spirit at hand. Is it actually, in the final sense, "the time of the end"? We cannot say. But we can echo, with longing hearts, the prayer of Evelyn Underhill, in her "Veni Creator," written for Pentecost Eve:

> When the morning wind
> Blows down the world, O Spirit, show Thy power;
> Awaken the dreams within the languid mind
> And bring Thy seed to flower.[2]

Notes

PROLOG

1. Douglas Steere, *Doors into Life* (New York: Harper and Brothers, 1948), p. 23.
2. Dorothy Ranaghan in *As the Spirit Leads Us,* ed. by Kevin and Dorothy Ranaghan, (New York: Paulist Press, 1971), p. 80.

THE CONFESSIONS

Epigraph: John K. Ryan, ed., *The Confessions of St. Augustine* (Garden City: Doubleday Image Book, 1960), p. 140.

1. *Confessions,* p. 17.
2. p. 82.
3. p. 111.
4. p. 176.
5. p. 202.
6. p. 216.
7. p. 220.
8. p. 224.
9. p. 43.
10. p. 255.
11. p. 46.
12. p. 254 f.
13. p. 253.
14. p. 369.

THE DESERT FATHERS

Epigraph: Helen Waddell, ed., *The Desert Fathers* (Ann Arbor: University of Michigan Press, 1957), p. 24.

1. *The Desert Fathers,* p. 9.
2. p. 56 f.
3. p. 43 f.
4. p. 160.
5. p. 20 f.
6. p. 63.
7. p. 66.
8. p. 72.
9. p. 95.
10. p. 96.
11. p. 154.
12. p. 51.
13. p. 119.
14. p. 61.
15. p. 45.
16. p. 24 f.
17. p. 22.

THE LITTLE FLOWERS OF ST. FRANCIS

Epigraph: St. Bonaventura, *The Life of St. Francis,* transl. by E. Gurney Salter (New York: Dutton, 1910), p. 322.

1. Bonaventura, p. 311.
2. p. 313.
3. *The Little Flowers of St. Francis,* transl. and ed. by Raphael Brown (Garden City: Doubleday Image Book, 1958), p. 81.
4. *Little Flowers,* p. 75.
5. p. 118.
6. p. 107.
7. p. 152.
8. pp. 143-147.
9. p. 54.
10. J. A. Dobson, *St. Francis, the Little Poor Man of Assisi* (New York: Fleming Revel, n.d.), p. 82.
11. Dobson, p. 83.
12. *Little Flowers,* p. 18.
13. p. 317 f.

THE IMITATION OF CHRIST

Epigraph: Albert Hyma, ed., *The Imitation of Christ* (New York: The Century Co., 1927), p. 33.

1. *Imitation,* tr. by George F. Maine (London: Collins, 1957), p. x ff.
2. p. 40.
3. p. 91.
4. p. 83.
5. p. 83.
6. p. 83.
7. p. 40.
8. p. 180 f.
9. p. 90.
10. p. 53.
11. p. 61.
12. p. 86.
13. p. 87.
14. p. 183.
15. p. 114.
16. p. 121 f.
17. p. 223.
18. p. 102.
19. p. 104.
20. p. 106.
21. p. 240.
22. p. 241.
23. p. 263.
24. p. 263.
25. p. 275 f.
26. p. 230.
27. p. 64.
28. p. 40.
29. p. 33.
30. p. 34.
31. p. 41.
32. p. 92.
33. p. 47.
34. p. 77.
35. p. 52.
36. p. 207.

FREEDOM OF THE CHRISTIAN

Epigraph: Martin Luther, *Christian Liberty,* transl. by W. A. Lambert and Harold J. Grimm (Philadelphia: Fortress Press, 1967), p. 30f.

1. T. G. Tappert, ed., *Selected Writings of Martin Luther* (Philadelphia: Fortress Press, 1967), p. 19.
2. *Christian Liberty,* p. 7.
3. p. 7.
4. p. 8.
5. p. 12.
6. p. 15.
7. p. 20.
8. p. 29.
9. p. 30.
10. p. 34.

THE INTERIOR CASTLE

Epigraph: Teresa of Avila, *The Interior Castle,* transl. by E. Allison Peers (Garden City: Doubleday Image Books, 1961), p. 105.

1. *Interior Castle,* p. 28.
2. p. 31.
3. *The Life of St. Teresa of Jesus,* transl. by E. Allison Peers (Garden City: Doubleday, 1960), pp. 105, 108.
4. Evelyn Underhill, *The Mystics of the Church* (New York: George H. Doran, n.d.), p. 179.
5. Underhill, p. 176.
6. *Interior Castle,* p. 40 f.
7. p. 47.
8. p. 80 f.
9. p. 81.
10. p. 84.
11. p. 107.
12. p. 127.
13. p. 213 f.
14. p. 217.
15. p. 220.
16. p. 229.
17. Transl. by H. W. Longfellow in *Masterpieces of Religious Verse,* ed. by J. Morrison. (New York: Harper and Bros., 1948), p. 39.

THE BOOK OF COMMON PRAYER

Epigraph: The Book of Common Prayer (New York: The Church Pension Fund, 1945), p. 18 f.

1. Book of Common Prayer, p. vi.
2. Robert E. L. Strider in William E. Cox, *The Heart of the Prayer Book* (Richmond: The Dietz Press, 1944), p. ix.
3. Percy Dearmer, *The Story of the Prayer Book* (New York: Oxford University Press, 1933), p. 50.
4. *Book of Common Prayer*, p. 17.
5. p. 19.
6. p. 92.
7. p. 595.
8. p. 594.
9. Dearmer, p. 11.
10. *Book of Common Prayer*, p. 38.

THE PRACTICE OF THE PRESENCE OF GOD

Epigraph: Nicholas Herman, *The Practice of the Presence of God* (Old Tappan, N.J.: Fleming H. Revell, 1958), p. 29.

1. *Practice of the Presence*, p. 9.
2. p. 30 f.
3. p. 11 f.
4. p. 34 f.
5. p. 35 f.
6. p. 19.
7. p. 61.
8. p. 47.
9. p. 47.
10. p. 36.
11. p. 48.
12. p. 31.
13. p. 43.
14. p. 48 f.
15. p. 42.
16. Joel 2:29.
17. John 6:45.

PILGRIM'S PROGRESS

Epigraph: John Bunyan, *Pilgrim's Progress* (Old Tappan, N.J.: Fleming Revel Spire Book), p. 256.

1. *Pilgrim's Progress,* publisher's note.
2. p. 13.
3. p. 39.
4. p. 57 f.
5. p. 58.
6. p. 73.
7. p. 79.
8. p. 112.
9. p. 90.
10. p. 90.
11. p. 49 f.
12. p. 141.
13. p. 142.
14. p. 209 f.
15. p. 210.
16. p. 211.
17. p. 211.
18. p. 212.
19. Isa. 66:2.
20. *Pilgrim's Progress,* p. 274.
21. p. 275.
22. p. 275.
23. p. 261 (altered).

THE JOURNAL OF JOHN WOOLMAN

Epigraph: The Journal of John Woolman (New York: Corinth Books, 1961), p. 185.

1. George Fox, *Journal* (New York: Dutton, 1949), p. 8.
2. *Journal of John Woolman,* p. 15.
3. p. 59 f.
4. p. 87.
5. p. 143.
6. p. 42.
7. p. 213.
8. p. 63.

9. p. 184.
10. p. 214.
11. p. 215.
12. Prov. 4:23.
13. *Journal of John Woolman*, p. 118.
14. p. 82.

FOR SELF-EXAMINATION

Epigraph: Søren Kierkegaard, *Concluding Unscientific Postscript,* transl. by David F. Swenson and Walter Lowrie (Princeton, N.J.: Princeton University Press, 1941), p. 542.

1. Walter Lowrie, *A Short Life of Kierkegaard* (Princeton, N.J.: Princeton University Press, 1952), p. 126.
2. Lowrie, p. 124.
3. *Concluding Unscientific Postscript,* p. 544.
4. James 1:23-24.
5. Søren Kierkegaard, *For Self-Examination,* transl. by Edna and Howard Hong (Minneapolis: Augsburg Publishing House, 1965), p. 10.
6. *For Self-Examination,* p. 14.
7. p. 23.
8. p. 28.
9. p. 29.
10. p. 29.
11. p. 37 f.
12. p. 39.
13. p. 50.
14. Luke 12:49.
15. Perry Lefevre, ed. *The Prayers of Kierkegaard* (Chicago: University of Chicago Press, 1956), p. 212.
16. Luke 17:14.
17. *For Self-Examination,* p. 82.
18. p. 83.
19. p. 85.
20. p. 86.
21. p. 89.
22. p. 92.
23. p. 100.
24. p. 101 f.
25. p. 104.

THE WAY OF A PILGRIM

Epigraph: The Way of a Pilgrim, transl. by R. M. French (New York: Seabury Press, 1965), p.17.

1. *Way of a Pilgrim*, p. 1.
2. 1 Thess. 5:17.
3. *Way of a Pilgrim*, p. 41.
4. p. 76 f.
5. p. 112.
6. p. 86.
7. p. 160.
8. G. P. Fedotov, ed. *A Treasury of Russian Spirituality* (New York: Harper Torchbook, 1965), p. 282.
9. *Way of a Pilgrim*, p. 186 f.
10. p. 227.

CREATIVE PRAYER

Epigraph: E. Herman, *Creative Prayer* (Cincinnati: Forward Movement Miniature, n.d.), p. 117.

1. Introductory Memoir in *The Secret Garden of the Soul* (London: Hodder and Stoughton, 1924).
2. Ibid.
3. Ibid.
4. *Creative Prayer*, p. 12.
5. p. 15.
6. p. 33.
7. p. 38.
8. p. 27 f.
9. *Creative Prayer* (London: Jas. Clarke and Co., 1921), p. 98.
10. *Creative Prayer* (Forward Movement Miniature), p. 78.
11. p. 110.
12. p. 111.
13. p. 111.
14. p. 94 f.
15. p. 94.
16. *Creative Prayer* (Jas. Clarke and Co.), p. 165.
17. *Creative Prayer* (Forward Movement Miniature), p. 70 f.
18. p. 72.
19. p. 114.

PRAYER

Epigraph: O. Hallesby, *Prayer,* transl. by C. J. Carlsen (Minneapolis: Augsburg, 1931), p. 12.

1. *Concordia Hymnal* (Minneapolis: Augsburg Publishing House, 1933), p. 315.
2. Joseph M. Shaw, *Pulpit Under the Sky* (Minneapolis: Augsburg Publishing House, 1955), p. 23.
3. *Prayer,* author's preface.
4. Isa. 65:24.
5. *Prayer,* p. 26.
6. p. 28.
7. p. 34.
8. p. 63.
9. p. 79.
10. p. 80 f.
11. p. 91.
12. Matt. 18:3.
13. *Prayer,* p. 171 f.
14. p. 173.

THE SCHOOL OF CHARITY

Epigraph: Evelyn Underhill, *The School of Charity* (New York: David McKay, 1934), p. 4.

1. Charles Williams, ed. *The Letters of Evelyn Underhill* (New York: Longmans, Green, 1953), p. 11.
2. Margaret Cropper, *Life of Evelyn Underhill* (New York: Harper and Bros., 1958), p. 9.
3. *Letters,* p. 44.
4. *School of Charity,* pp. 27 ff.
5. pp. 45ff.
6. pp. 66 ff.
7. p. 67.
8. p. 3.
9. pp. 96 ff.
10. p. 86.
11. p. 92.
12. pp. 92 ff.
13. p. 104.

14. p. 109.
15. p. 108.
16. p. 108.

LIFE TOGETHER

Epigraph: Dietrich Bonhoeffer, *Life Together,* transl. by John W. Doberstein (New York: Harper and Row, 1954), p. 28.

1. *Life Together,* p. 8.
2. p. 8.
3. p. 13.
4. p. 13.
5. *Letters and Papers from Prison,* ed. by Eberhard Bethge (New York: Macmillan, 1967), p. xiii.
6. Ibid., p. xiv.
7. *Life Together,* p. 19 f.
8. p. 47.
9. p. 62 f.
10. p. 68 f.
11. p. 66.
12. p. 79.
13. p. 79 f.
14. p. 92 f.
15. p. 112.
16. p. 115.
17. p. 120 f.
18. Matt. 7:14.

EPILOG

1. Ps. 73:25-26.
2. Evelyn Underhill, *The Mount of Purification* (New York: David McKay, 1960), p. 151.